GAMES

for

FUNDRAISING

WILLIAM N. CZUCKREY

Pineapple Press, Inc.
Sarasota, Florida

Inquiries should be addressed to:
Pineapple Press, Inc.
P. O. Drawer 3899
Sarasota, Florida 34230

LIBRARY OF CONGRESS
CATALOGING IN PUBLICATION DATA

Czuckrey, William N., 1916-
    Games for fundraising / William N. Czuckrey
        p. cm.
    Includes index.
    ISBN 1-56164-074-3 (alk. paper)
    1. Games.   2. Fund raising.   I. Title
GV1201.C98   1995   95-20296
790.1'5--dc20   CIP

First Edition
10 9 8 7 6 5 4 3 2 1

Design by Carol Tornatore
Composition by Sheila and Edward Johnston
Printed and bound by Quebecor/Kingsport in Kingsport, Tennessee

NOTE TO READER:

Some of the building projects described in this publication require the use of tools and machinery that should be used with care. Common-sense safety precautions should be taken to avoid the risk of injury. The reader accepts the risks involved when engaging in building projects.

Some of the games described may be prohibited by local or state law. Consult the proper authorities before choosing games for your event.

TABLE OF CONTENTS

INTRODUCTION

Fairs and carnivals used to be a special world of their own, and one of their main characters was the professional "barker" enticing us into his game with the familiar cry, *"Step right up, ladies and gentlemen!"*

These days, the person manning the booths and chanting, *"Tell ya what I'm gonna do!"* is more likely to be one of your neighbors or a member of your church or club. From apple-cheeked kids to snow-topped grandparents, everybody gets into the act to have a good time and raise money for their church, fraternal group, school, sports or charity group, or any other cause you can think of. Excitement is high, because people feel good when they are involved in a cause that means something personally. It's even better when their efforts produce great results.

The purpose of this book is to help you get the best results from your next fundraising event. You'll learn a wide assortment of simple and profitable games that are easy to put together and carry out, and which are guaranteed to bring in a decent profit for your group. The games and activities presented here can be used by anyone — whether it's the Little League team putting on a neighborhood carnival to raise money for uniforms, or the Junior League staging a glamorous evening to raise money for charity.

Despite the growing popularity of this type of fundraiser, there is little information on how to actually get it going. A flood of questions usually accompanies the decision to try a fair or carnival: How do we plan it? What are the jobs that need to be done and what kind of outside help, if any, will we need? Can we build the games ourselves, or should we rent them? Is it expensive? How many people will be needed to run the games?

With this book in hand, you won't need to rely on hired "professionals" who end up with most of the profits, or on willing but inexperienced (and soon overwhelmed) volunteers. Only games and activities that have been thoroughly tested and proven are included in this book, along with plenty of suggestions for planning a successful event. Your own creativity will make these ideas work for your particular group.

One word of caution: In some areas, state or local regulations limit or prohibit any form of "gambling," which may apply to some of the games described here. Often the procedures of the game can be adjusted to conform to the law; for example, if it is illegal in your state for money to be awarded as a prize, players can win tokens based on a point system, and exchange the tokens for merchandise. Be sure to check carefully with the proper authorities in your state and county before planning your event.

The games and events described in this book fall into three major categories: games of chance and fortune, games of skill, and auctions and raffles. Games of chance include wheel games, "slot machine" look-alikes, the ever-popular bingo, dice games, and card games. Games of skill described in this book include target games played with darts, dart guns, or pop-guns, and hoop games. Both these categories fit into the familiar "carnival," "fair," or "honky-tonk" type of event. Auctions and raffles, on the other hand, are more sophisticated and less common, but still can be very successful if managed correctly.

Many of the games in this book will be familiar to you, and some will not. But all are designed to give both pleasure and profit. When you come right down to it, that's the whole point: to build cooperation and self-esteem, to get people involved, to have fun, and to produce fabulous funds! So let's get started, and good luck in your next event.

GENERAL SUGGESTIONS

There are three ways to set up how people at the event pay for games: cash, chips, or tickets. With the cash method, people place bets or buy chances in a game using actual coins or bills. A second method is to have people purchase chips of different denominations upon entering the fair, and use those chips to play the various games. The third method is to sell tickets for a set amount each (or at a discount for several tickets bought at once) and have each game accept one or more tickets as the admission price. The price for each game may vary, but a common fee is 25 cents per try. For games involving betting, people would simply use multiple tickets for larger bets.

If the cash method is used, it is wiser for each operator to wear a change apron than to have a change box lying around near the game. The operator should have enough change on hand so as not to have to inter-

rupt the game to go for more; once a momentum of play is established with customers, a break will slow down the action for a significant time. A volunteer "gofer" (go-for) should be assigned to regularly check with the operator of each game during the event to see if more change or supplies are needed, so that the operator doesn't have to interrupt the game.

When actual cash is used in a game, such as quarters, the operators should be furnished with a roll of quarters ($10), ten single dollar bills, and one five-dollar bill. Where dollar bills are being used to pay for playing the game, the operator should start with ten singles, one five and one ten-dollar bill. (Note that, in both instances, the starting cash pool is $25; careful records should be kept by the "house" so that correct profits can be calculated later. When an operator needs more change, for instance, he or she should exchange a large bill for smaller ones. This also prevents large amounts of cash from accumulating in the booths.)

There should be clear signs in and around the booths indicating the cost of the play and what sorts of prizes are being given for winning.

The types of prizes to have on hand will vary for each game. For most games, especially those in which a player is guaranteed a prize for every play, the prizes should be very inexpensive — the sorts of toys and trinkets you might find at a flea market. There should be a sprinkling of slightly more valuable prizes on hand to spark interest in winning. The number of prizes to have on hand for each game will vary according to the number of people attending, the difficulty of the game, and the popularity of the game, but a good rule of thumb is to have an initial stock of prizes and have two or three replacement sets of prizes on hand.

Operators who can establish a rapport with passers-by to entice them to participate will do much better business than those who simply wait for players to come to their game. People make the difference between some games working right and making money and others gathering dust or rust! A busy game will tire out an operator within two hours, so arrangements should be made ahead of time for replacements to be ready to rotate as needed.

WHO'S GOING TO DO WHAT TO GET THIS FAIR OFF THE GROUND?

As you ask that question, you stare out at a sea of empty stares or eyes cast to the floor to avoid meeting yours. Almost no one wants to volunteer at first, even though just a few minutes ago, people were full of ideas and enthusiasm about how "This could be the best fundraiser that our group ever put on!" Bringing talk to fruition takes good leadership skills as well as time and real effort. Somehow, eventually, things start to fall into place. Fumbling hands and puzzled brains replace the windy words. Somewhere in the group emerges an unheralded artist, a talented carpenter, a surprising "hawker," a gofer crew, a general maintenance gang, and a bunch of amateur operators who don't know beans about running any game, but who are chomping at the bit to learn how. What they lack in skills and know-how they make up in enthusiasm and creativity. Maybe the end product is a bit crude in appearance, but it's functional and operable. And the pride in their accomplishments is bursting from every wrinkle in their paint-spotted clothes. And that's the way many fundraising projects start their creative and exciting journey to building money-mountains. Of course, most of the games described in this book (or variants of them) can be rented or purchased from central supply houses (see Sources and Resources).

HOW TO USE THIS BOOK

Each game begins with a general descrip-tion of how it is played, how many people are needed to run it, and the estimated profits at a typical fair. Then, except for a few cases of games that are considered too complex to build (such as Roulette), a list of materials and step-by-step instructions are given for constructing the game, including how to set it up and what kind of supplies and prizes to have on hand. The resource section offers some ideas for finding inexpensive prizes, chips, and other supplies needed to run these games successfully.

TOOLS AND SUPPLIES

Those with home workshops or access to building tools will probably have everything they need; following is a comprehensive list of tools that will serve for every game described in this book:

Awl
Brushes, various sizes for lettering and painting
Chisel
Drill, electric, with various bit sizes
File, round
Framing square
Hammer
Hole punch
Mat knife
Measuring tape, steel
Pencil (for marking)
Pliers: general, channel-lock, needle-nosed
Protracter
Router
Sandpaper, various grades
Saws: sabre, jigsaw or scroll, cross-cut
Scissors
Screw drivers, regular and Phillips
Wood glue (for any jointed wood surface regardless of whether it is nailed or screwed)
Wrench, crescent
Yardstick

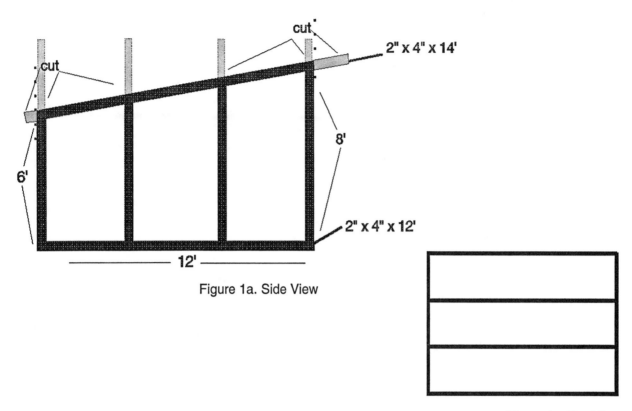

cut

cut

2" x 4" x 14'

8'

6'

2" x 4" x 12'

12'

Figure 1a. Side View

Figure 1c. Top View

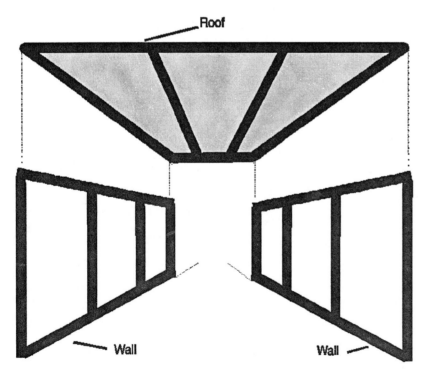

Roof

Figure 1b. Front View

Wall

Wall

Figure 1a and b. Booth construction.

Other general supplies you should have on hand:

> Glue: general purpose (such as Elmer's)
> Graph paper
> Paint: glossy, various colors
> Rubber cement
> Stapler
> String: thin nylon and kitchen

Many games, especially those in which the players throw balls, darts, or other "missiles" at a target, need to be set up in a booth enclosed on three sides to protect passers-by from stray flying objects. The sides and back can be enclosed with sheets of canvas, heavy fabric, or sturdy plastic. A booth constructed of wood is durable — lasting many years. A more lightweight booth can be built out of PVC pipe. Although one person can build the booth, assembly requires a few strong people.

BUILDING GUIDE FOR THE GAME BOOTH (SEE FIGURE 1)
(Instructions are for a 12-ft booth)

Materials Needed	
Lumber	
10	2" x 4" x 8'
4	2" x 4" x 12'
6	2" x 4" x 14'
Lag bolts	
6	¼" x 3"
Screws (for wood)	
56	3½" x #12
Tarp (or canvas or heavy plastic)	
2	8' x 12'
1	12' x 12'

Building the Walls:
1 To make one side of the booth, lay one 2 x 4 x 12 (for the bottom) on the ground with four 2 x 4 x 8's (for a wall) perpendicular to it (as shown in Figure 1a). Measure and mark 8 ft on one of the outer 2 x 4 x 8's (since 2 x 4 x 8's are not necessarily 8 ft long). Measure and mark 6 ft on the other outer 2 x 4 x 8.

2 Using one of the 2 x 4 x 14's, lay it diagonally across the top of the 2 x 4 x 8's, and carefully place on the 8-foot and 6-foot marks (this creates a sloping wall). The 14-ft will intersect the inside 2 x 4's; mark the intersections.

3 Now mark the 14-foot piece where it intersects the two outer 2 x 4's. (You should have a total of six marks.) From the high sides of the marks, use a framing square to draw a straight line. Adjust your circular saw to the angle on the edge of the 2 x 4. Cut the pieces at the marks. Using these pieces as a pattern, cut a second set for the opposite wall. Screw the wall pieces together. (Screws are used so that disassembly is possible.)

Building the Roof:
1 Lay two 2 x 4 x 12's parallel on the ground. Cut four 2 x 4 x 14's the same length as the 14 ft top of the walls, *less* 3 inches (this is to make up the difference in measurement of the front and back 2 x 4's). Place, evenly spaced, between the 12-ft pieces. Screw together (see Figure 1c).

Assembling the Roof and Walls:
This may require a couple of people.
1 Stand the walls up. Hoist the roof and set on the walls. Attach roof with the lag bolts, three per side, evenly spaced.

2 Taking care that the walls are perpendicular to the roof, measure down 6 ft from the corner of the roof (on the 6-ft piece on the back of the corner of the roof) and mark. From the same corner, measure across 4 ft (on the roof 2 x 4). Place a 2 x 4 x 8 in between these two marks. (This will create a 4 x 6 x 8 triangle.) Do the same on the other side. Screw the 2 x 4's diagonally from the

low side of the wall (6-ft mark) to the roof (4-ft mark). This is to give the structure some rigidity (Figure 1b).

3 Finally, the entire structure is covered with a tarp (or canvas or plastic). To attach the tarp (canvas or plastic), staple in place.

Note: The inclusion of tables or other structures in the booth is at the discretion of the group holding the event.

GAMES *of* CHANCE *and* FORTUNE

Introduction

Games of chance have been around for centuries—even millennia. There are records of dice games, for example, dating from some of the earliest records of civilization. Thanks to the lure of Lady Luck, who draws the gambler on with her enticements, games of chance will always be popular.

Carnivals, fairs, and "game nights" (Las Vegas Night, Monte Carlo Night, etc.) all borrow from the basic games played in most casinos. Other games are homemade copies of professional carnival games, and still others spring from the ingenuity and imaginations of those involved in creating the event.

Following is a brief description of some of the games included in this section. Most of these games are easy to build and operate and many, of course, are also available for rental. Whichever avenue you choose, it will be an adventure!

Two of the best-known fundraisers in this category of games are the **Big-Six Wheel** and **Bingo**. Since the Big-Six Wheel is usually played with money as the pay-off, take care to substitute prizes other than money if laws require it in your area. This is usually done by awarding points or "units" for a win. These may take the form of designated rolled-ticket stubs, specially printed paper, or cardboard slips designating the winner's prize amount.

These tokens are then exchanged for merchandise designated as requiring the specified number of tokens. Either way, there is always much excited play on this wheel and it is always a good source of income for the group.

Bingo, on the other hand, is generally accepted as a game where money prizes can be awarded legally. This is also the most popular and probably the greatest money producer of any fundraising game. With very few exceptions, Bingo brings in money regularly but in varying amounts, depending on how it is run. Because it can be adapted to so many areas and methods, both indoors and outdoors, most groups rely on it either as an occasional fundraiser or as a permanent part of their program. The equipment and manpower required depend upon the nature and extent of the game being conducted, which ranges from the simple one-card-per-game structure to the very sophisticated super-hall containing over a thousand players at a time.

Although these two games are usually the most successful, depending on location and circumstances, other games might do as well— or even better. There are no hard and fast rules about which games succeed best; many times it just takes some trial and error.

Craps: This fast, loud, and very exciting game of rolling dice and betting on the outcome has been and still is one of the most popular and productive activities around. A real pulse-popper, it should always be included in every fundraiser's repertoire, if at all possible. Naturally, check out permits, allowances, and local attitudes before including Craps in the game line-up. Many modifications can be employed to make the game conform to local requirements without infringing on the basic concepts. Directions for building a simple Craps table are included with the description of the game.

Blackjack: Many fans of this game believe that this is one of the few games that is most favorable to the player. It may be. What is certain is that many wait for the turn of each card with avid anticipation. As in every game, the returns to the "house" depend to a great extent on the person conducting the game. Knowledge of the odds, card counting, and other strategies of the game are all important in determining its profitability. It's definitely not for every fundraising endeavor, but it's a well-known and popular game.

Although **Roulette** is usually found at most "Las Vegas Night" fundraisers, and is a favorite game in casinos internationally, it does not seem to catch on much in general funding endeavors. Probably this is because most people frequenting these "home-grown" money-making operations find it difficult to understand the numerous ways of betting in this game. Except for the aura of sophistication this game lends to a gambling-type event, it probably will not pull in impressive profits.

The **Sunshine Bandit** is a direct take-off on the slot machines. A newcomer, and tried in only a few areas, the Sunshine Bandit already elicits a positive reaction from players. Designed to accommodate up to eight players at a time, it retains the suspense and anticipation of the regular slot machine. Its three colorful spinning wheels have a hypnotic effect on passers-by, luring them to play. The odds are very favorable to the "house" and the game is simple to operate. Because this game is also

very new, and not available from any dealer, extensive diagrams and instructions for building it are included. A promoter of any fundraising enterprise should be amply rewarded by having some handy member of the group take on the building of this project. (This is one of the games originated and developed by the author.)

Under and Over 7 is a deceptively simple game with a seemingly questionable profit margin for the operator, which tends to make it attractive to game players. Strictly an illusion! In reality, the game is quite profitable to the outfit running it and is simple to build and operate. Definitely a plus for the profit-seeking fundraiser.

The **Horse Race Romp** is a departure from the traditional Horse Race Game or Horse Race Wheel usually found at fairs and carnivals. Even though this game requires considerable equipment and substantial set-up, it inevitably attracts good crowds and players. Its many colorful objects plus the intense action prove to be an irresistible attraction to just about everyone. This game is usually found on cruise ships and at indoor events, but it can be easily adapted to an outdoor event. With proper handling, this game can prove to be an excellent moneymaker.

Fortune-telling games have a wide appeal, and many forms of it are used in fundraising events everywhere. An enjoyable instant-fortune-telling card game called **Happenings** has been experimented with in some areas and has evoked a positive response. Because it does not require extensive instruction, and depends on the card-reader using his or her own interpretation, it lends itself to a great measure of credulity. Also, because fees can be varied according to the complexity or length of the reading, it is a good prospect for pulling in considerable funds. A full Happenings deck is illustrated in Chapter 5 along with some sample readings. This game was developed and tested by the author and is included with the full belief that it can be a creditable fundraiser.

CHAPTER 1

▼

WHEEL GAMES

With their exciting spinning, whirring, flashing, and creeping, wheel games are always major moneymakers. All of them are easy for the customer to play, simple for the operator to run, and, in most cases, quite possible for ambitious fundraisers to build. Because there are more kinds of wheel games around than it is possible to include in this book, some of the most popular and newer versions will be presented with guidelines on their operation and expected return as well as how to build some of them. The wheel games that will be described are:

Big Six Wheel
Money Wheel
Dottie Wheel
Roulette
Various Carnival Wheels
Sunshine Bandit

BIG SIX WHEEL

How It's Played:

A betting board with six dice symbols (from 1 to 6) is laid out in front of the players, on which they place bets of cash or chips on their favorite number or numbers. Only one operator is required to run this game unless more than one betting board is used. The operator tries to get as many bets down as possible before spinning the wheel. Winners are paid off on the basis of one-to-one: that is, the prize won equals the amount that was bet. For example: One player bets three chips on #5 and another player bets two chips on #3. The wheel is spun and stops with the pointer on the space having two five-spot dice and one three-spot die. The operator places six chips next to the bet of the player on #5 and two chips next to the bet of the player on #3. That completes that spin. Because it's so easy to understand and play this game, and because the odds seemingly favor the player, this game usually gets plenty of action. The fact is that the wheel does a nice job for the operator; it is not unusual to expect up to 40 cents of every dollar played to stay with the game as profit.

BUILDING INSTRUCTIONS FOR BIG SIX WHEEL (SEE FIGURE 2)

Materials Needed	
Plywood	
1	4' x 8'(½")
Lumber	
1	2" x 4" x 8'
1	1" x 3" x 8'
1	1" x 2" x 8'
Copper tubing	½" ID
Leather (thick) or Plastic (pliable)	
1 Strip	1½" x 6-in

Bolts/Nuts		
1	¼" Threaded bolt, 4" long	
2	¼" Machine bolts, 4" long and 2 nuts	
1	½" Full-threaded axle bolt, 8" long and 4 nuts	
Washers		
4	to fit axle bolt	
3	¼" Plain metal	
Screws (for wood)		
2 Flat-head	2¼"	
Nails		
19 Common	3"	
54 Finish	4" (Optional)	
Rubber cement		
String/pencil		

Creating the Wheel:

1 Mark and cut plywood into a 3-ft square.

2 Mark center of the plywood square. This can be accomplished by drawing diagonal lines from corner to corner. The center is where the lines intersect.

3 Cut the plywood square into a 3-ft circle. The lines for this or any of the circles can be drawn a number of ways. One method is to tap a nail or tack on the center of the plywood. A string (sufficiently long) with a pencil at the end is attached to the nail and each of the circles is drawn. Another method that works even better is to take a yardstick or a longer piece of flat lumber (lattice works very well) and drill a hole in it near one end (for the center hole). Other holes may be drilled at the proper distance from the center for the other desired circle diameters. Place the first hole of the yardstick on a nail tacked into the center of the plywood. With pencils in the other holes, draw the circles as the yardstick is rotated.

4 Decide whether you plan to notch the outer edge or use a smooth edge with protruding nails. Cutting notches is more laborious and difficult to do. If you decide to cut notches, be sure each one is oriented to the center of

each die (see illustration). If you decide to use a smooth edge, be sure to place the nails so that they protrude about an inch or so from the edge evenly, all the way around (see instructions, # 6).

5 Using a protractor, divide the surface into 54 equal spaces (6.66° each). To mark off notches, draw a circle about 1 inch from the outside edge. Determine the center of each die space along this line and make a mark. Continue around the circle. With a straight edge (or ruler), connect the marks. When you have completed marking the notches, cut them out with a jig saw.

6 To use the nails, drive finish nails into the perimeter of the circle at each marked line (created from the template) so that they protrude evenly — about 1 inch.

7 Draw eight more circles on the wheel. Use the outer six for the "three-dice" lines. The other two will be used for the decorative area and the center axle-housing area.

8 Paint the wheel a bright color such as orange or yellow, paying special attention to the edges. Allow to dry. Paint the dice marks as shown in the illustration in a dark or contrasting color. Paint the inside circles using decorative or flashy artwork — let your imagination soar.

Creating the Wheel Stand and Pointer Assembly:

1 The stand for the wheel is made from a 6-ft section of 2 x 4 (for the upright), two 3-ft sections of 1 x 3 (for the base), and four 24-inch 1 x 2 (for the angled supports). Cut these pieces from the existing lumber.

2 Rout out the centers of the two base pieces (1 x 3 x 3) so they will fit snugly crosswise.

3 Angle cut the four supports (1 x 2 x 24's) so they fit neatly between the base pieces and the upright (2 x 4 x 6).

4 To make the pointer assembly, cut two 2 x 4 x 8-inch pieces (from the 24-inch lumber remaining after cutting the upright). Cut a notch in the center of the wide (4-inch) side

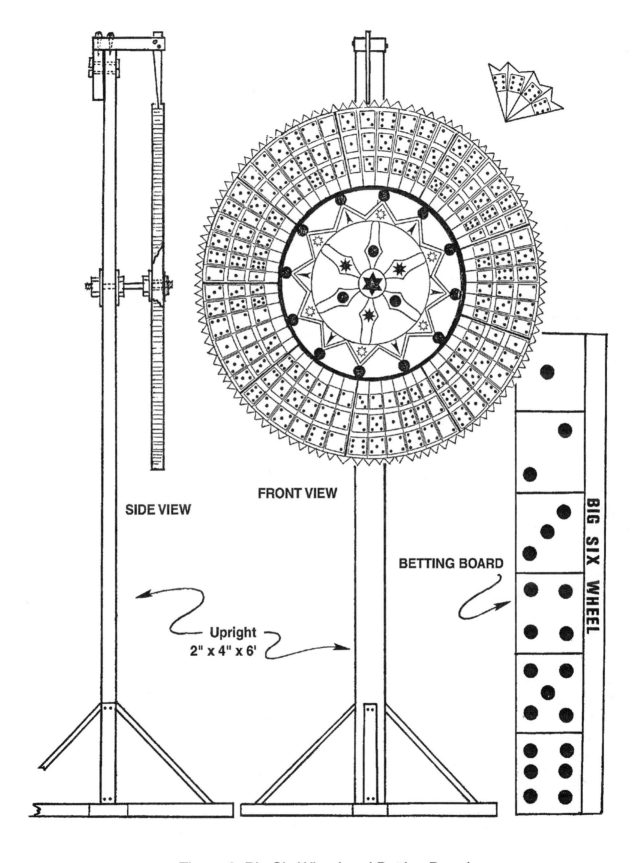

SIDE VIEW

FRONT VIEW

BETTING BOARD

Upright
2" x 4" x 6'

BIG SIX WHEEL

Figure 2. Big Six Wheel and Betting Board.

of a 2 x 4 x 8-inch piece. The notch should be deep and wide enough to insert the leather or plastic strip (pointer). One end of the leather (or plastic) should be flush with the top and sides of the wood. The other end will stick down far enough so that the leather (or plastic) will strike the notches (or nails) on the outer edge of the wheel. Drill a ¼-in. hole on the side of the block and through the pointer. Insert a ¼" x 4" threaded bolt through the hole and an appropriate-size plain washer on the exposed threaded end; fasten with a ¼-in. nut.

Assembling the Unit:

1 On the top of the 2 x 4 x 6, fasten the other 2 x 4 x 8-inch piece with machine bolts, nuts, and washers, forming a flush end (4" x 4"). Then screw the pointer assembly to the 6-ft upright, positioning so that the pointer end extends toward the side of the upright where the wheel will be placed.

2 Lay this assembly on a bench or table, pointer side up, and place the wheel so that the outer edge will be in contact position with the pointer. To help position the wheel axle, drive a nail through the center of the wheel before placing on the upright. Once the correct position is determined, press hard. This will create a slight indentation on the upright, marking the position for the axle center. Drill the hole in the upright for the axle bolt that will hold the wheel to the upright. Drill another hole in the center of the plywood wheel the same diameter as the copper tubing.

3 Attach the wheel to the upright using the axle bolt, washers, nuts, and copper tubing (as shown in the diagram). The copper tubing, when placed correctly, will act as a bearing.

4 With the upright still on the bench, take the crossed bases that have been routed and fit together and nail the base assembly to the upright using 3 common nails. This will hold the assembly steady enough to set the upright on the floor.

5 Attach the four 1 x 2 x 24 supports using common nails.

Making the Betting Board:

1 To make the betting board, enlarge the diagram in Figure 2 onto an 8' x 18" piece of plywood.

2 Paint the board (to match the wheel) and place on a sturdy counter or table.

MONEY WHEEL GAME

How It's Played:

This wheel has 50 spaces with $1, $2, $5, $10, and $20 bills, and in two of the spaces a Joker or two $20's (see Fig. 3). In order to off-set potential problems with shortages and theft, use "funny money" for the wheel display and use actual cash for the pay-outs. The betting board is laid out with similar money denominations. For the wheel you will need twenty-four $1 bills, fifteen $2 bills, seven $5 bills, four $10 bills, two $20 bills, and two Jokers or two $20 bills ($40 pay-out).

This game also works on a one-to-one payoff. *For example*: One player puts a $2 bet on the $10 bill on the betting board and another player bets $2 on the $5 bill on the board. The operator spins the wheel and it eventually stops with the pointer on the $10 space. That player with the $2 bet on the $10 space wins $20 and the player with the $2 bet on the $5 bill loses his bet. If bets were placed on any other numbers, they would be lost, too.

This is usually a popular game and attracts players in good numbers. This game should easily earn anywhere from 35 to 40 cents on every dollar played. Its construction is similar to the Big Six Wheel.

BUILDING GUIDE FOR THE MONEY WHEEL (FIGURE 3)

Materials Needed
Same materials needed as for the *Big Six Wheel* (pp. 9-12).

Building Directions
Construct the wheel and attach to an upright

using the building directions for the *Big Six Wheel (pp. 9-12)*. Instead of cutting grooves along the outside edge of the wheel, use nails as in the alternate design for the *Big Six Wheel*.

DOTTIE WHEEL GAME

How It's Played:

This is a new game in the fundraising arsenal. While it appears to be a variation of the Big Six Wheel, there are some significant features that affect the profit percentages and make for a simpler design. There are only 30 spaces on this wheel as compared to 54 on the Big Six, and one win on a space as against three ways on the other. It should bring a higher percentage of profits on the dollars played on it. A return of 40 to 50 cents on every dollar played could be realized.

BUILDING INSTRUCTIONS FOR THE DOTTIE WHEEL (FIGURE 4)

Materials Needed and Building Directions
Same as for the *Big Six Wheel (pp. 9-12)*. You can either cut grooves or use nails for this wheel.

Figure 3. Money Wheel Game and Betting Board.

Figure 4. Dottie Wheel and Betting Board.

ROULETTE

How It's Played:

One of the older games around, roulette still attracts plenty of action and excitement. The spinning bowl in which the metal ball is tossed, along with the colorful and unique betting panel, make this game attractive, if a little intimidating to many people. The broad range of betting possibilities can be confusing and deters some people from playing the game. Once players become familiar with how to bet, however, they usually become constant or even avid players of the game.

The betting table is divided into two sections known as the "inside" section and the "outside" section (see Figure 5). The "inside" section consists of all the individual numbers and the "0" and "00." All the rest of the betting table is known as the "outside." There are 36 individual numbers and a "0" and "00" that can be bet as a single number with a chip or chips. If any one of those 38 "numbers" are bet and win, the payoff is 35 to one.

To bet two adjoining "numbers," one places the chip or chips on the line joining the two numbers. If one of these two numbers wins, the payoff is 17 to one. There are 63 ways to win a two-number bet.

To bet three numbers at a time, one places a chip or chips on the line intersecting the "0" and "00" and joining on the number "2," or places a chip or chips on the line between any of the numbers in the column from "1" to "34" and the "outside" layout. A win on any of those three numbers pays off 11 to one. There are 15 ways to bet three numbers.

To bet four numbers at a time, one places a chip or chips on the intersection of four numbers. This is confined only to the numbers from "1" to "36." There are 22 ways to bet on four numbers at a time, and the payoff is eight to one. There is only one way to bet five numbers with one bet, and that is to place the bet on the dividing line between the "0,00" numbers and the "1, 2, 3" numbers. The bet is

placed on the line dividing the "inside" and "outside" sections. This win pays off six to one but is not recommended for gambling. Six-number bets can be made by placing the bet on the dividing line of the "inside" and "outside" section on the number lines connecting to the line dividing the two sections. If any of the six numbers in this combination win, the payoff is five to one. There are 11 ways to bet this combination.

Betting 12 numbers at a time can be done in six ways. Each of the long number columns (1 to 34, 2 to 35, or 3 to 36) is a 12-number bet. The bet is placed either at the bottom of one of the three columns or in one of the three sections labeled first 12, second 12, and third 12. If the winning number comes up in any of these sections, the payoff is two to one.

There are six ways to bet 18 numbers with one bet and they are almost self-explanatory by

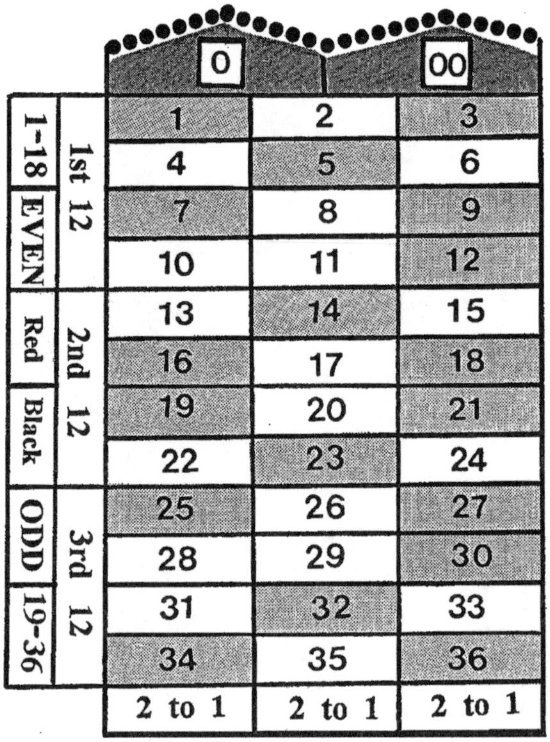

Figure 5. Roulette Betting Board.

the wording of the outside panels. If the winning number comes up in these combinations, the payoff is one to one.

A supply of different-colored chips should be available, because each player is sold a supply of chips with a color different from that of any of the other players. The chips are sold by the "stack" with a stack containing 20 chips. A predetermined value is given to the chips and has to be posted so that players are aware of the cost. Now, the chips have no monetary value but can have an arbitrary value assigned to them for the purpose of determining the means of winning or losing at these games. Professional casinos figure the "take" or profit at better than five cents on every dollar bet; that figure is probably the same for nonprofessionals. Obviously this game requires an operator who is very familiar with the game. This game does not need a special booth and can be set up on a table in a space that will allow enough people to crowd around, with the wheel and betting board placed so that people not playing can pass by without disturbing the players. A roulette wheel is too complicated to build and can be rented fairly inexpensively along with a betting board.

If desired, the betting board can be easily built using a 48" x 72" piece of 3/8" plywood sanded smooth and painted as shown in Figure 5. Numbers should be large and easy to read; they can be hand-painted or you can use stick-on numbers available at art-supply outlets. The shaded areas are traditionally in green. Set the board on a sturdy table large enough to hold the wheel as well.

VARIOUS CARNIVAL WHEELS

How They're Played:

Carnival wheels are similar to the Big Six Wheel and the Money Wheel, in that they have a betting board and pay-off based upon the pointer stopping on a winning number. They differ in numbers of sectioned spaces and in various ways the sections may be graded, depending on where the pointer comes to rest. As an example, looking at the wheel that has 36 numbers (see Fig. 6), note that each number has a spoke at the center, plus spokes on either side of the center where the pointer could also come to rest. The operator would pay off a prize of lesser value if the pointer was on these side spaces, and a better prize if the pointer was on the center dot. Similarly, looking at the carnival wheel with 15 numbers, note the divisions at the rim of each number.

With so many more numbers to contend with for a win in comparison with the Big Six Wheel, why would many players bother to play these carnival wheels? The answer rests with the type of prizes that can be won. In contrast to less expensive prizes that are usually stocked in the wheel games with a small range of prize-winning numbers, the prizes in these carnival wheels are usually of good quality and impressive value—such as clocks, statuary, or small electronic items, which may be solicited from local merchants. The operators familiar with these wheels know that a player seldom wins a prize with all those numbers. As a rule, there is less action on these games than some of the others, but enough to warrant having them if they are available or if someone has the ambition to build them.

BUILDING GUIDE FOR CARNIVAL WHEELS (FIGURE 6A)
Materials Needed and Building Directions
Refer to materials list for the *Big Six Wheel (pp. 9-12)* with the exception of the lumber and fasteners necessary to construct the upright. Decorate wheels as shown in the figure, or with your own variations.

BUILDING A STATIONARY WHEEL (FIGURE 6A, TOP)
Materials Needed and Building Instructions
Following the directions as given with the *Big Six Wheel (pp. 9-12).*

Cut a 36" plywood circle. From the remaining plywood, cut out an arrow 2" x 34". Insert the copper tube into the pointer to act as the bushing. (In this wheel assembly, the pointer moves and the wheel is stationary.) Assemble with the axle bolt, nuts, and washers.

BUILDING A MOVABLE WHEEL (FIGURE 6A, BOTTOM)

Materials Needed and Building Instructions
Follow the directions as given for the *Big Six Wheel (pp. 9-12)*.

In this case, the wheel moves and the pointer is stationary. Since this wheel sits on a table, construct a base assembly from a circular 36-in. piece of plywood. The two plywood circles are attached with the axle bolt assembly as previously described. The pointer assembly is attached to the lower (nonmoveable) plywood circle with the 4" x 4" corner brace.

SUNSHINE BANDIT

How It's Played:

This game is very similar to a slot machine. Although the game is simple enough to be run by one operator, it probably is better to have two. With two operators, each can watch and service half of the betting board. This game is best housed in a booth. To operate it, one spins the three horizontal wheels individually, in the same direction or in opposite directions, and stops the three wheels simultaneously by applying the hand brake. The betting board allows up to eight players at a time to bet. Each individual space on the board lines up with three symbols on the wheels. Since it is based on the slot machines, the type and number of symbols on each of the three wheels conforms fairly closely to a typical three-wheel slot machine. The payoff panels on

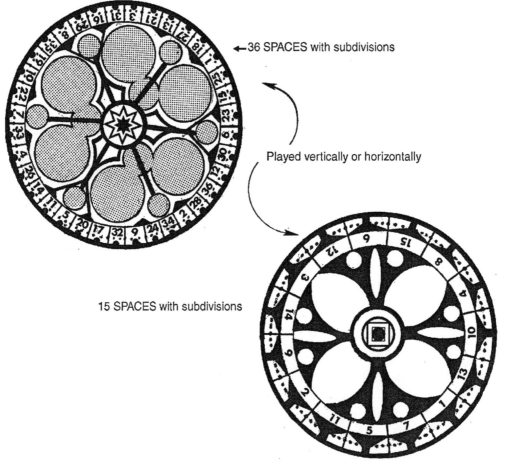

← 36 SPACES with subdivisions

Played vertically or horizontally

15 SPACES with subdivisions

Figure 6. Various Carnival Wheels.

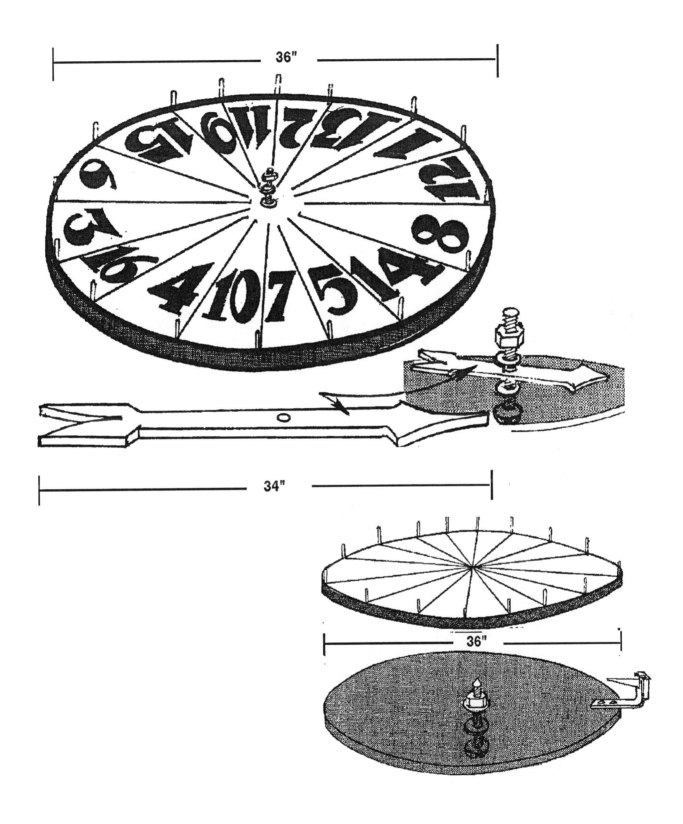

Figure 6a. Carnival Wheels — Stationary Wheel (top) and Movable Wheel (bottom).

the sides indicate the winning combinations and what they pay.

Because this is a fairly new entry into the wheel game world, the returns have not yet been firmly established, but, from all indications so far, it should return about 50 cents on every dollar played.

Although the Sunshine Bandit takes more than the usual time and material to build than other wheel games, it is fairly compact, interesting, and has the potential of being a consistent moneymaker. It certainly attracts a crowd wherever it is used. It's simple to operate and fits into just about any game plan.

BUILDING GUIDE FOR THE SUNSHINE BANDIT (FIGURES 7A-G)

Materials Needed

Plywood		
4	4' x 8' ($^3/_8$")	
Lumber		
1	1" x 2" x 8'	
Wood screws		
3	$^1/_2$" x #8	
6	$^3/_4$" x #8	
4	1" x #8	
Threaded rod		
1	$^3/_8$" x 18"	
Washers		
7	$^3/_8$"	
Nuts		
14	$^3/_8$"	
Flange, floor		
1	$^3/_8$"	
Copper tubing		
4	$^1/_2$" x $^3/_8$" ID	
Nails, finish		
60	#8d (optional)	
Strap hinge		
1	3"	

Creating the Basic Unit:

1 Cut three 36-in. and two 42-in. diameter circles from the plywood. Remember to mark the centers (see *Big Six Wheel, pp. 9-12,* for directions).

2 Using one of the 36-in. circles, mark 20 equal sections (18^0 each). Then, draw a second circle with a diameter of 35 inches.

3 Start with any two adjacent points on the outside perimeter of the 36-in. circle. Draw an angle backward to the center of the line drawn for the 35-in. circle. Cut these pieces out with a jig saw to create the notches. Continue around the circle until you have notched the entire circumference. Use this circle as a pattern for creating the two other notched circles. Alternatively, you can use nails as the stoppers, by driving 20 nails into the circumference of the circle so that only $^1/_2$ in. to $^3/_4$ in. protrudes. (Be sure that they protrude evenly.)

4 Drill a hole in the center of the three 36-in. circles and in one of the 42-in. circles. Insert a piece of $^3/_8$ in. copper tubing in each one. File down the copper tubing until it is almost flush with the top and bottom of each board. Make the hole in the copper tubing a bit bigger by drilling with a 25/64 drill bit.

5 Cut a 1 in. wide by 3½ in. deep notch into the 42-inch circle (with the hole). (This will be for the brake; see later.)

Creating the Wheel Strips:

1 Using medium-weight cardboard or sturdy paper, cut three long strips about 110 in. long and 5 in. wide. Cut away 2-inch sections to leave at least 5 flaps equally spaced (see Figure 7e). Paint with large symbols as illustrated. (The strips in Figure 7e are not drawn to scale; they will actually be wider than they are high.) Figures 7f-g provide actual-size diagrams for copying onto the strips — or create your own special symbols. Line up each of the symbols either within two nails or in a groove around the circle. Attach each strip to the underside of each of the 36-in. wheels using glue. Be sure to have ample glue on the flaps to secure the strips.

2 Prepare another 44 in. x 3 in. strip for the numbers, with at least three or four flaps. Divide the strip into eight 5½-in. sections. Number from 1 through 8. Glue onto the 42-in. wheel (the one with the hole in the center), about 1 in. from the outer edge and

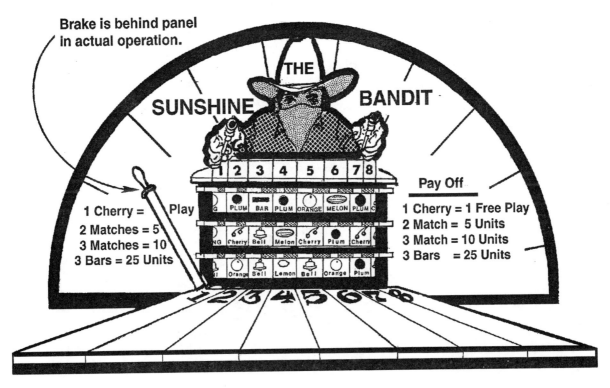

Figure 7a. Sunshine Bandit.

with the one about 10 in. around from the notch.

Assembling:
1 Starting with the 42-in. circle (without the hole in it), attach the ³/₈-in. floor flange in the center with ½ in. wood screws. Screw the ³/₈ in. threaded rod into this. Onto the threaded rod, place two nuts. Be sure the top nut is about 3 in. from the base; tighten together.
2 On top of this, place a washer and the first wheel, checking to be sure that there is about 1/8 in. clearance between the symbol strips and the base. Then, place another washer and two more nuts on the rod. Tighten the lowest nut "hand-tight" to the washer. This should allow the wheel to spin freely. The second nut is then tightened to the first. Proceed in this manner for the other two wheels.
3 The other 42-in. circle is then put on the rod; a washer and nut is placed on top to finish

the assembly. Cut off any excess threaded rod.
4 Measure the distance between the 42-in. circles, and cut the three 1 x 2's to this measurement. Screw the 1 x 2's into the 42-in. circles with 1-in. wood screws to divide the circle into thirds.
5 Cut another 1 x 2 to 18 inches. This will serve as the brake. Place into the notch on the top piece of plywood, so that the bottom of the 1 x 2 rests on the lowest 42-in. circle. Place the strap hinge between the 1 x 2 and the lower circle, and screw on with four 1-in. wood screws.

Constructing the Betting Board and Backboard:
1 Cut a 48" x 60" piece of plywood for the base. Mount the wheel assembly flush with the back edge and center (3" from each edge), using six ¾-inch wood screws.
2 From the other piece of plywood, cut a half circle with a 3-ft radius for the backboard. Measure the height and width of the wheel

assembly and cut a notch of these dimensions from the center of the flat side of the backboard.

3 Cut four 6-in. right triangles from the plywood. Glue the flat sides together, in pairs to form supports of double thickness.

4 Mount the backboard behind the numbers (1–8) on the top of the 42-in. wheel. Support it on each side with a triangle, and screw them into the base and backboard.

5 Paint the backboard and the baseboard.

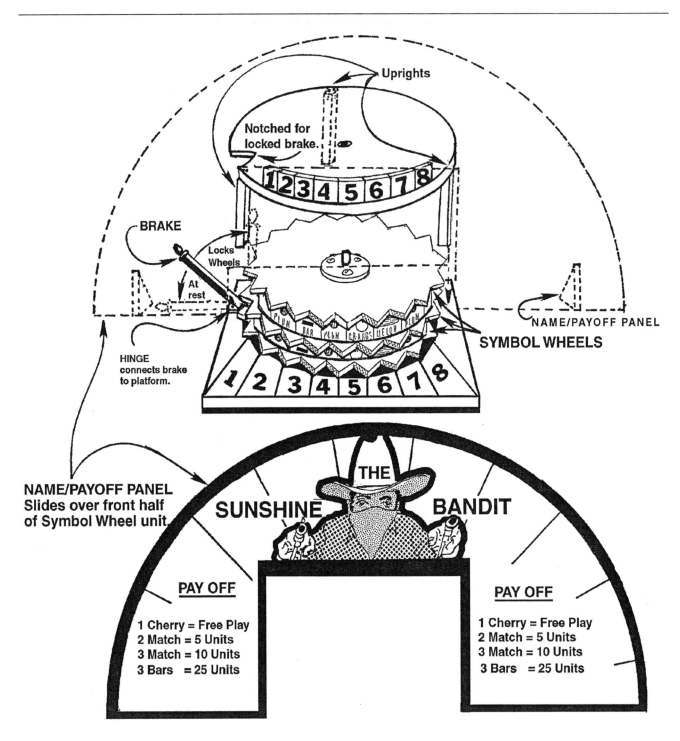

Figure 7b. Sunshine Bandit — Exploded view

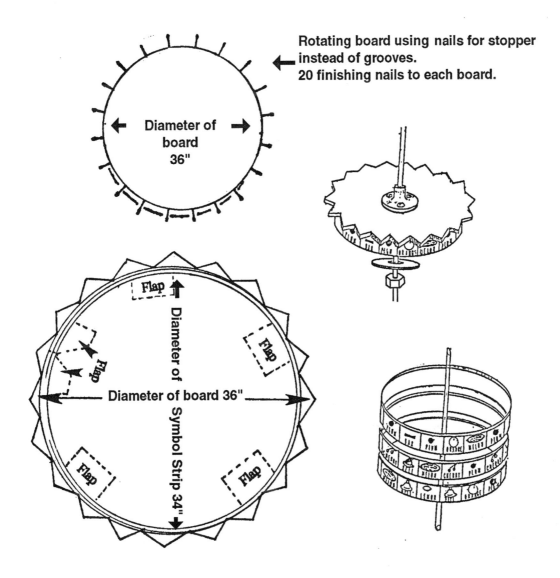

Rotating board using nails for stopper instead of grooves.
20 finishing nails to each board.

Diameter of board 36"

Flap

Diameter of board 36"

Diameter of Symbol Strip 34"

Flap

Flap

Flap

Flap

Figure 7c. Sunshine Bandit –Wheel Dimensions.

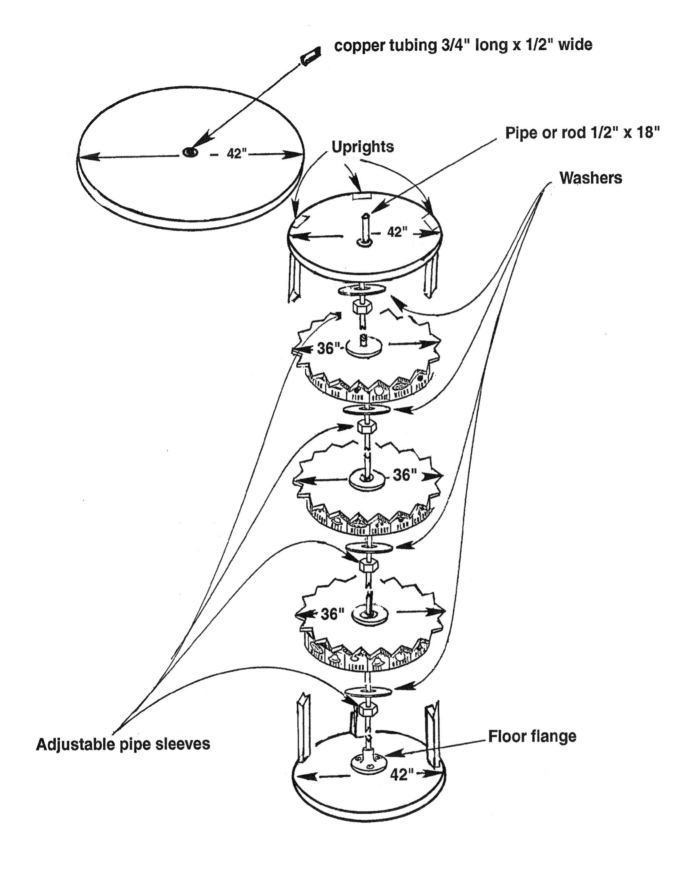

Figure 7d. Sunshine Bandit–Exploded View of Wheel Assembly.

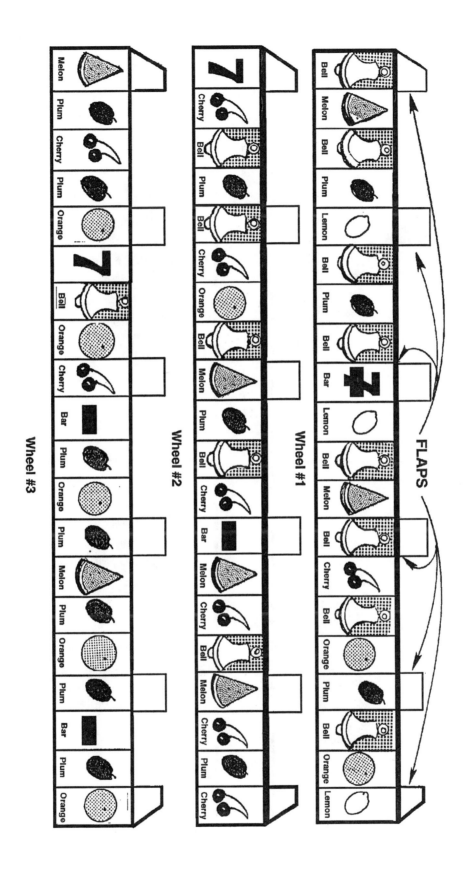

Figure 7e. Sunshine Bandit–Wheel Symbol Strips.

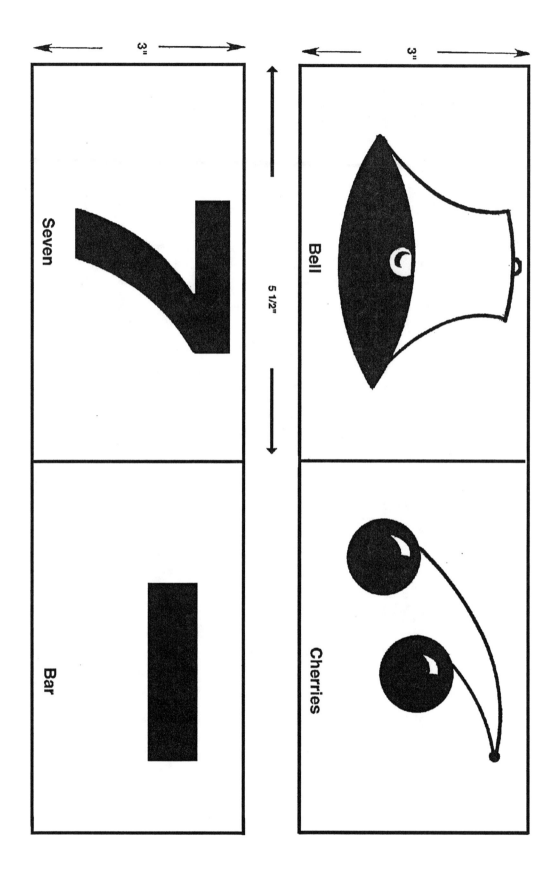

Figure 7f. Sunshine Bandit–Symbol Patterns.

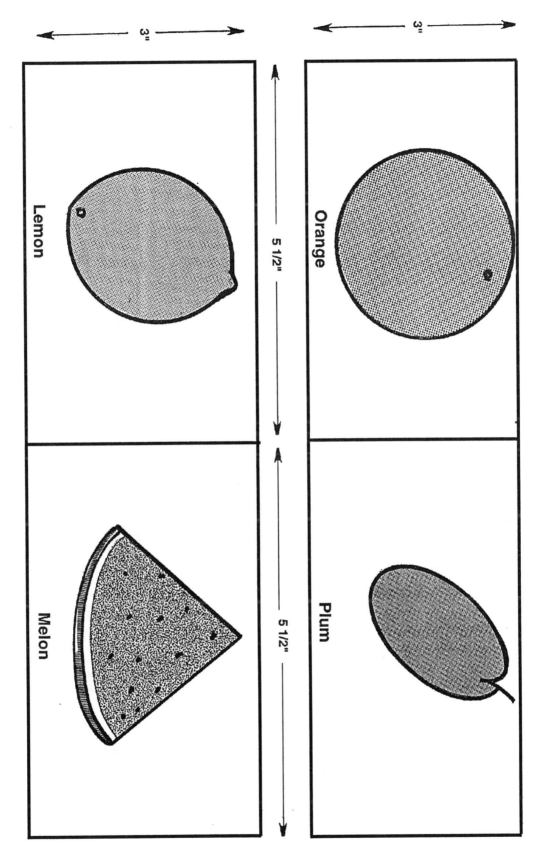

Figure 7g. Sunshine Bandit–Symbol Patterns.

CHAPTER 2

BINGO

Bingo is by far the champion of fundraising games. Bingo can be played in many ways, and the returns will vary according to what kind of bingo is played. But whatever way it is set up, bingo is always popular and, if conducted properly, can be an unquestioned leader in fundraising. Bingo is so entrenched in the daily activities of so many people outside of special fundraising events that it has become an institution in its own right. Yet, even though it exercises such influence, and functions as a standard weekly game for many organizations throughout the country, it is still run as a regular feature in many carnivals, fairs, bazaars, Las Vegas Nites, and other fundraising events.

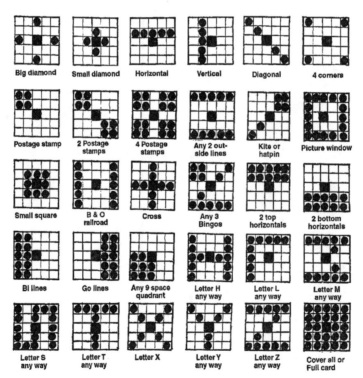

Figure 8. Bingo Winning Patterns.

How It's Played:

For a fee, each player is issued one or more game boards (cardboard or paper) with 25 squares, each numbered at random between 1 and 75. The operator, either by manually turning a cage or by operating a blower cage, retrieves numbered Ping-Pong or plastic balls one at a time and calls out the number. Players place markers on the numbers that appear on their game boards and can win by getting a sequence of numbers in a line horizontally, vertically, or diagonally — or in a number of other patterns (see Figure 8). The phrase "Jackpot" means that all of the numbers on a card must be covered in order for it to be a winner. When a player has a winning combination, he or she calls out *"Bingo!"*

Proceeds collected for each game are divided up, with a certain percentage or flat fee going to the "house." More than one person can win in a game. If this occurs, the portion of the prize allocated to the players is divided equally between each winner. There are many ways to win at bingo, and anyone can learn to play easily.

If the "house" is an establishment that runs a bingo game regularly, they may use semipermanent cardboard bingo cards for these events. More and more groups, however, are relying almost entirely on paper strips to play bingo and eliminating the cardboards. The pay-for-each-game method of playing bingo is not the greatest money-producing method, but it is the most practical way to conduct the game at special events because it allows a continuous operation with fluctuating attendance (in these situations, people will be joining and leaving the game continuously). Usually, players are offered cards at a set price per card or a discount for multiple purchases, for instance, ten cents per card or three cards for a quarter. Rarely will a player take only one card.

The house is expected to furnish certain objects for the game, and the players are expected to have the rest. If the game is being played on cards, the house usually has a supply of cardboards and plastic or cardboard markers the players can use to cover the numbers on the card. If the house uses paper strips, the players purchase "daubers" to mark the numbers on the paper. The dauber is a metal tube containing a colored liquid which passes through a sponge-type tip at one end of the tube onto the paper, marking the space but leaving the number visible (like a type of transparent highlighter pen). Plastic or cardboard markers can be used both on the cardboards and on the paper, but daubers cannot be used for the cardboards. Regular bingo players usually own their own plastic chips and markers and, in many cases, also own magnetic sticks (wands) to pick up the metalized chips.

In some ways, this is the most difficult type of game to run. Even the smallest game being operated requires at least three people: the Caller, the Collector and Payoff person, and the Treasurer or Bookkeeper who keeps track of the income and pay-out.

Before dissecting the "regular" bingo game, which is slightly different but will quickly be recognized by veterans of the game, it might be well to view a "special" version of the game that some groups use fairly often, even those that conduct ongoing games each week of the year. These games are usually referred to as "marathon" or "limited players" games. In the parlance of bingo, it is referred to as a "package" deal because a set number of games are included with specific payoffs; any other specials are also part of the total that is purchased by the players. Marathons typically include a meal, limit the number of players, and set the event to be played on a day (usually a Saturday or Sunday) a few weeks ahead. Meals are either "box lunch" or cooked on the premises by the members. The group usually advertises the affair several weeks before the scheduled day and sells tickets during that period. When the quota is reached, sales stop. Following is a sample ad:

HOLY ONE CHURCH BULLETIN
MARATHON BINGO TO BE HELD
APRIL 31
AT CHURCH HALL
Tickets limited to 100 players.
Get your tickets early at the Church Hall
any day between 10:00 A.M. and 8:00 P.M.
Cost of ticket $25.00 each for the
total package, which includes:
Delicious Spaghetti Dinner
35 Bingo Games!!
12 Early Birds — $20.00 Each
20 Regular Games   "$25.00 "
3 Jackpots   "$100.00 "
Free Coffee & Doughnuts !
Dinner starts at 5 P.M. and
Bingo starts at 6 P.M.

The organization in this example can anticipate that their gross receipts will be $2500. The cost of the prizes will be $1040. Approximate cost for the meal is figured at about $2 per person, which makes the total for the food $200. That brings the total expense to $1240 for prize payoffs and food, for an estimated profit of $1260.

Sometimes "specials" are included in the package, but if they are not, then it's almost certain that at least two specials will be played during the regular program at an extra cost for purchasing strips for the specials. The strips are normally three bingo cards on a strip of paper and are sold as one strip or a set of three strips at a discount. As an example: One special strip costs $1. Three strips may be purchased for $2. There are always players who buy many more of the special strips, on the theory that the more strips they play, the better chance they have of winning. No one tries to convince them otherwise.

Following through on the premise that two "specials" will be played at this affair, how much more will they net? Based upon past

experience, they can anticipate that almost all the players will buy the discount strips and a few of them will buy even more. Thus, they can figure another $250, which should bring their balance to this: (The following balance sheet does not include utility costs or use of facilities since it is assumed the building is owned by the organization. Nor are extra profits figured in from sales of extras such as cigarettes, candy, etc.)

Ticket income:	$2500.
Income from specials:	$250.
Gross income:	$2750.
Prize payouts:	$1040.
Specials payout:	$200.
Cost of dinners:	$200.
Total Expenses:	$1440.
Estimated profit:	$1310.

This example indicates the potential of an average-sized marathon game.

SETTING UP THE GAME

In permanent locations where bingo is played on a regularly scheduled basis, the games are usually more elaborate and sophisticated, the equipment is electronically operated, and prizes are substantially greater. With the temporary arrangements typical of bazaars, fairs, and other fundraisers, the simpler type of bingo is normally played; this means using manual equipment rather than electrical, individual game collection and payoffs rather than set prizes, and fewer people involved in the operation of the games. In some cases, the electrical equipment is rented for the occasion; alternatively, the permanent bingo setup of an organization may be temporarily converted to the carnival or fair venue.

Figures 9 and 10 show some examples of electrical and manual equipment. The cost of purchasing an electrical ball selector and flashboard – about $1000 as of this writing – is probably prohibitive to most small groups. In manual models, the ball cage usually comes with wooden balls with burnt-on numbers. It would be a complicated process to try to build this cage, but the cost of renting or even purchasing this cage with the wooden balls is comparatively minimal (around $100). It is readily available in most populated areas around the country and if not, it can be easily purchased, or even rented, by mail. (See Resources for suggested sources.)

The flashboard is another matter. Because of bulk and costs involved, renting or purchasing might be prohibitive. The manual model portrayed (see Fig.10) was designed and built under just such a circumstance. Standard lumber was used for the frame and supports,

numbered boards were cut from tile board, large drinking straws were glued onto the numbered boards which were, in turn, slipped on the rods in their proper order. The necessary washers, screws, and nails were purchased to put the entire project together and a bit of paint added to finish the job. The total cost for materials for this manual flasher did not exceed $50, and even this modest cost could be modified by using less-expensive materials. For instance, where the six horizontal pieces of lumber were 2 x 4 x 8, a change to 2 x 2's (with the same lengths) instead of 2 x 4's would reduce the cost somewhat. Also, instead of using tile board for the numbered boards, 4" x 4" posterboard or cardboard could be used.

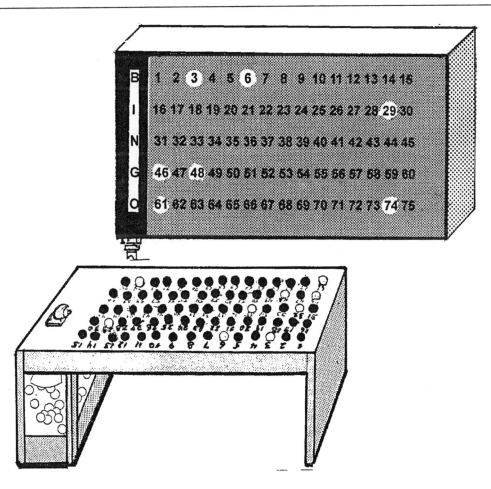

Figure 9. Electronic Bingo Equipment.

BUILDING GUIDE FOR BINGO MANUAL FLASHER
(FIGURE 10)

Materials Needed

Lumber
3	2" x 4" x 8'
4	1" x 4" x 8'
1	1" x 3" x 8'

Dowels, wooden
15	1/8" x 26" x ½"

Washers, steel
150	1/8"

Wood screws
30	2¼"

Tile board
75	4" x 4" pieces (approx. 9 sq. ft.)

Nails
5	#6d

Drinking straws, jumbo, 20
White glue

Creating the Flasher Lettering:

1 On the seventy-five 4 x 4 pieces of tile board, paint (or stencil) the numbers 1–75, using a contrasting color from the tile board. Cut the drinking straws into seventy-five 3-inch pieces. After the numbered tiles have dried, glue the drinking straws to the center back of the tiles, taking care to mount them vertically.

Creating the Flasher Assembly:

1 From the 2 x 4 x 8 lumber: cut two pieces 71¼ in. Drill 15 holes completely through one of the 71¼ in. pieces (this will be the top) and halfway through the other (this one will become the bottom). The first hole is 3¾" from the edge with each subsequent hole 4¼ in. apart.

2 From 1 x 4 x 8 lumber: cut four pieces 64 in.

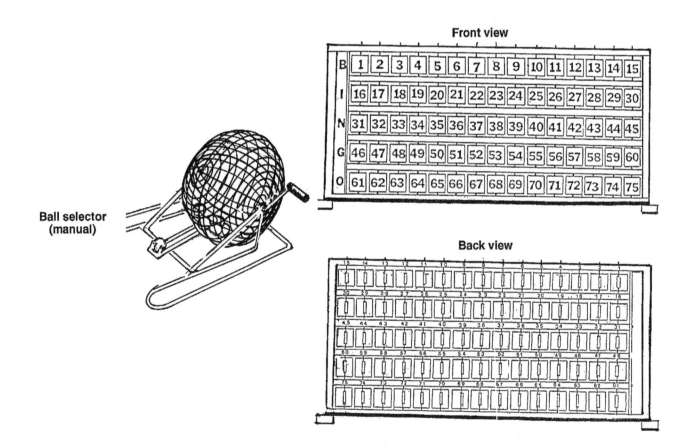

Ball selector
(manual)

Figure 10. Bingo Manual Flasher.

Drill 15 holes completely through the four pieces. In this case, the first hole is 2½" from the edge with each subsequent hole 4¼ in. apart. These will be the separator boards.

3 From 1 x 4 x 8 lumber: cut two pieces 24¼ in. Attach one to the other perpendicularly to the edge (forming a letter "L") with 5 finish nails. Paint the word BINGO vertically (as shown) on the face of the board.

Assembling:

1 From 2 x 4 x 8 lumber: cut two pieces 24¼ in. Drill and screw together the bottom 2 x 4 x 71¼ with the two side 2 x 4 x 24¼ and the BINGO title board. Glue the 15 wooden dowels into the holes in the bottom 2 x 4 x 71¼ and allow to dry. Place a washer over each dowel. Place the last set of numbers (61–75), one on each dowel, followed by another washer. Then place one of the separator boards over the dowels; drill and screw into place with 2 wood screws, one on each side. Continue in this fashion to the top row. After the top row is in place, mount the top 2 x 4 x 71¼ to the sides.

2 Cut 1 x 3 x 8 lumber into two pieces, 24 in. long. These will be the frame supports. Mount the two 1 x 3 x 24 frame supports perpendicular to the bottom piece of 2 x 4 x 71¼, one on each side.

3 Number the separator boards just above the individual tiles (on the back side of the flasher). Again, these numbers can either be stenciled or painted on to the wood framing.

Although this operation takes some time to prepare and assemble, the result of careful construction is a flashboard that can be used for many years.

Besides the ball selector and the flashboard, other supplies are required for bingo. The hard cardboard or paper bingo cards that are sold to the customers, plus the markers (usually cardboard) that are used to cover numbers on the boards, can usually be found in local outlets or bought through the mail from numerous wholesale outfits (see

Sources and Resources). Permanent bingo establishments sell plastic or magnetic chips.

PERMANENT BINGO SET-UP

Bingo games run on a regular basis, week after week, by a group in a permanent structure can be quite profitable. Unless the operation is run in a shoddy manner or the neighborhood deteriorates rapidly with a bad element taking over the area, bingo virtually guarantees success. In every state where bingo is allowed and where it is played fairly, it has paid off more mortgages, built more structures, made more groups viable, and given more people pleasure than any other endeavor.

Success does not come automatically, however. Because this game appeals to so many people and is so easy to play, it may seem to be simple to run. Actually, a successful bingo operation takes a lot of work and sharp supervision. Everything is important and needs constant attention: the equipment, the workers, the customers, and the surroundings.

An example of the importance of these factors is a fraternal organization in Florida that had been running a clean bingo for several years and doing quite well with it. The game had been instrumental in paying off the mortgage on their property, which was near the center of the city. The proceeds from bingo enabled them to refurbish the entire interior and put in a modern bar, a clubroom with padded chairs and sturdy modern tables, a fully equipped office, and even their own printing facilities.

It seemed the good times would never end. But eventually gangs of kids began roaming in the neighborhood. Pocketbooks were being snatched. Cars parked for bingo were being broken into. Players going home after the game were pistol-whipped. A custodian of the fraternal hall was beaten senseless with a baseball bat by an intruder at noon time when the custodian left a door open while cleaning the hall. In a matter of 6 months the attendance of players dropped to such a low level that it was impossible to continue. Several years have passed since that happened and the group has tried to revive the game several times, but to no avail. This true story shows how important locale can be to the success of a regular bingo game.

Perhaps the most important element in the business of playing bingo is the operators. Almost without exception, for the games we are talking about here, all workers must be volunteers of, or have some affiliation with, the sponsoring organization. Most state laws prohibit any workers to be paid from the proceeds of bingo games. How is it possible to have such dedicated people run these paying enterprises every week, year after year, with such zeal and without any compensation? Many people truly believe in the cause their organization stands for, to the extent that they thrive in giving whatever they can in time and effort for the organization. A few others may not be so motivated. The key to handling volunteers with tact and motivation usually depends upon the leadership qualities of the game captain or chairman. Of course, not all game leaders make good decisions, but if the crew includes some sensible, stable workers, usually the game turns out fine. How a chairperson runs the bingo game with the crew often makes a big difference on the income that results. To make that point clear and, at the same time, demonstrate the type of income that may be expected from a regular weekly scheduled bingo game, two actual operations will be reviewed (names and details have been changed to protect their privacy).

The first group we'll call the Knights of Virtue, a fraternal group. The chairperson of the fraternal group is a man of average intelligence and character but obstinate and uncomfortable in sharing ideas with his committee. He is a hard worker and does more than his share for the organization. The second group, which we will call La-Dee-Dah Estates, is a community club of semi-civic origin. The chairperson of this group is a woman who runs

a low-key operation with a minimum of reporting of the game and a close following of her personal friends on her committee. She becomes very emotionally upset when anyone questions her operation. Both of these leaders are aware of the state laws as related to bingo. The man follows them carefully. The woman doesn't. This is the kind of game each conducts.

Over a period of about five years the fraternal group ran their games fairly well along these lines with periodic changes in size of prizes and other factors warranted because of changes in the law or pressure of competition. The Knights of Virtue also issued identifying cards, perforated into three sections. The top and bottom sections of the card are torn off and retained by the game's operators and the middle section is retained by the player. The middle section is displayed near the player's cards so it can be checked by the game personnel as to the correct number of cards being used by the player at any time. The top section, which indicates the number of cards paid for as a "package" in the regular games, and the bottom section, which identifies the number of cards paid for in the package as early birds, serves to double check the expected collection for each game. The community club had no such system.

Though each group had roughly similar player attendance, they handled the records and actual play in a dissimilar manner. The fraternal group assigned two people to collect the money prior to both the early bird and regular games. The chairperson and his assistant, who is also the recorder/bookkeeper, collected the monies and entry stubs during the games and also filled in as callers if necessary, and there were at least four floor workers circulating to call back winning cards, answer questions, and do whatever else had to be done to keep the players happy. There were also workers in the kitchen to serve the food and drinks and to fill in where necessary.

The records of the fraternal group show that their income ranged from a low attendance of about 80 players, bringing in a net income of about $300, to a medium attendance of 100 players, which netted them $500-$600, to a good attendance of about 115 players, which brought in $1200-$1300. One of their highest nets for a night of bingo was $1800.

The Community Club operation, on the other hand, has no standard agenda of games and prizes being paid. Their general program charged $1 admission for every player and a certain amount per card the player bought. There were no early bird games. They played their regular games, specials, and one jackpot (which normally paid $100) on a combination of cardboard card games and paper strip games. Here is an example of the average cost of play: A player paid her $1 for entry and selected 15 cardboard cards for each of the cardboard games. She bought three paper strips for two of the paper games and two paper strips for the third paper game. She paid $8.25 total. Depending on the decision of the chairperson, each regular game will pay anywhere from $15 to $25. Specials will pay off at $25 to $30. There were no circulating committee members on the floor during the game, the chairperson collected all the money and paid out all the prizes, made out the records herself, and gave a very brief oral report to the club each month. Call-backs on winning bingos were done by any player near the person having the winning card. The chairperson herself participated in playing all the games. Because of the fluctuation of players in the area for seasonal reasons, she claimed she must hold a reserve during the high income season to compensate for the low income time and therefore managed to break even each year. No profit and no loss.

This sample comparison shows how identical laws in the same state and a relatively comparable attendance can produce entirely different results.

OTHER CONSIDERATIONS

The "Bingo Split Pay-off Chart" (Figure 11)

was developed to help simplify the process of determining the payoffs for "split" games. Much time is lost and considerable confusion reigns when a number of players win a game at the same time. That's called a "split" game and means the prize has to be divided equally among the winners.

EQUIPMENT

Whether it be a manually operated squirrel cage with wooden bingo balls or an electronic "state-of-the-art" bingo machine, if it's not working right it's big trouble! Few things can be more frustrating than an equipment failure in bingo with a hall full of players talking, shouting, and stamping in impatience while the bingo workers are scurrying around trying to get things going. Everything mechanical, audio, and electrical needs a constant and thorough check before a game starts and during the interval between games. Also, the balls should be periodically washed if they are the plastic type. Oil from the hands and dirt coats the surface which can affect the ball action. Moving and storing the equipment should be carefully done since some parts can be broken or damaged easily.

The income of regular bingo games can be supplemented by the accessories, food, and drinks that can be sold to the players during the games. New gadgets pertaining to bingo are always coming out, besides those already available such as magnetized "wands," chips, pillows, bags, and charms. It all contributes to profit.

THE PLAYERS

Finally, let's look at the source – the many players that come up with the bucks over and over to make bingo the great fundraising goldmine that it is. Players come in all shapes and moods but they have one thing in common: an addiction for bingo! Some attend the game at least once a day every day of the week. A few attend a game more than once a day. Like

PRIZE AMOUNTS

Number of Winners	$15.00	$20.00	$25.00	$30.00	$35.00	$40.00	$45.00	$50.00	$100.00
1.	15.00	20.00	25.00	30.00	35.00	40.00	45.00	50.00	100.00
2.	7.50	10.00	12.50	15.00	17.50	20.00	22.50	25.00	50.00
3.	5.00	6.65	8.35	10.00	11.60	13.35	15.00	16.65	33.35
4.	3.75	5.00	6.25	7.50	8.75	10.00	11.25	12.50	25.00
5.	3.00	4.00	5.00	6.00	7.00	8.00	9.00	10.00	20.00
6.	2.50	3.35	4.15	5.00	5.85	6.65	7.50	8.35	16.65
7.	2.15	2.85	3.60	4.30	5.00	5.70	6.40	7.15	14.30
8.	1.85	2.50	3.10	3.75	4.45	5.00	5.60	6.25	12.50
9.	1.65	2.20	2.75	2.35	3.90	4.45	5.00	5.55	11.10
10.	1.50	2.00	2.50	3.00	3.50	4.00	4.50	5.00	10.00

Figure 11. Bingo — Split Payoff Chart

people everywhere, they like attention and comfortable surroundings. For many, bingo is the only recreational outlet they have.

Disruptions of the game do happen. People faint, have seizures or heart attacks or slip and fall. Callers should be prepared for these emergencies and keep as calm an atmosphere as possible during the occurrence as workers attend to the victim. If possible, the caller should continue calling numbers and try to have the situation return to normal quickly. Dwindling attendance can be cured sometimes by aggressive advertising or a sweetening of prizes. Normally, attendance doesn't fluctuate very much unless the location is a seasonal area or the operation becomes intolerable for some reason.

CHAPTER 3

▼

DICE GAMES

"*C'mon you bones, baby needs a new pair of shoes!*" Dice rattlers throughout the country will recognize that chant. The urge to talk to those dotted squares as they click and tumble in a sweaty palm next to the player's ear is almost compulsive. Few games evoke stronger emotions than do the dice games. There's something about those galloping cubes that triggers such excitement from players. Several dice games will be introduced, but craps or, as some like to call it, bank craps, will be given step-by-step clarification since, despite the enthusiasm the game causes, many people do not completely understand the rules or all the ways craps can be played.

Most fundraising events involve several games using dice, but only the most popular — and the most lucrative — will be dealt with in this chapter.

Games described in this chapter:
Craps or Bank Craps
Horse Race Romp
Under and Over 7
Chuck-A-Luck Game

CRAPS OR BANK CRAPS
How It's Played:
First, let's look at the inside of the craps table (see Fig. 12). The spaces outlined with the black lines and the messages and numbers inside might seem confusing. It helps to visualize the lined and printed parts as three separate sections. The center part has a series of panels that seem stacked on top of each other; the top panel is printed with "Seven" in large letters and some kinds of odds in smaller letters on each side. At the bottom panel of this center section, a message in large letters says "Any Craps" and on each side of this message are smaller letters and numbers indicating the odds. Imagine this center section to be the body of a bird. The two identically shaped sections on each side would then be the wings. Make the top of the center section the head of the bird and the bottom the tail.

In the casinos, it takes four individuals to run a craps game. The boxman sits or stands at the center of the table at the head of the bird as described above. His job is to take care of the money and chips and to make sure the game is played correctly. The stickman stands opposite the boxman at the table and handles the dice and the bets in the center (the body of the bird). Two stand on each side of the boxman. Their job is to collect the losing bets and pay off the winning bets on their own side of the table (the wings). They also make change for the

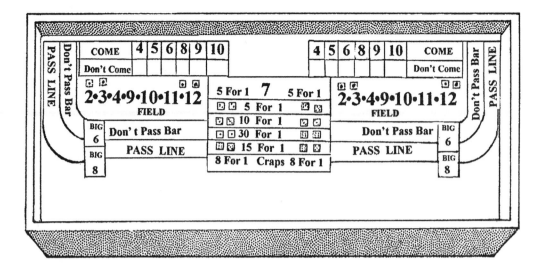

Figure 12. Craps Table—Betting Diagram

players. Players play from either end of the table.

Now, the betting. On each wing, the lowest panel has a message "Pass Line" and curves around to the top of each wing. This usually gets a lot of play from neophytes because it's easy to understand and bet on. When is it time to place a bet? You see the stickman pushing dice toward a player at the end of the table. That means the last play is over and a new player is going to roll the dice. This is a good time to put your bet on the Pass Line, if that is what you want to bet on. If the player throws a 7 or an 11, you win. If a 2, 3, or 12 come up, you lose. If a 4, 5, 6 or 8, 9, 10 comes out, that becomes the Pass Line Point, which means that particular number must come up again on the subsequent rolls to win; if a 7 comes up before the particular number comes up, you lose. The bet on the Pass Line pays off at one-for-one.

Come Bets are placed in either of the wings where the message "Come" appears (which is the fourth space up from the bottom). It is placed on the space only after a point has been established, which means after a new player has thrown the dice for his first time and neither a 7 nor 11 nor 2, 3, or 12 has come

up but a number in the 4, 5, 6 or 8, 9, 10 group is established as a point to be made. A Come Bet can be made any time after a point has been established. Once the bet is made on the established number, only that number will win if it comes up and will lose if a 7 comes up before it does. Come bets pay off at one-to-one.

The Don't Pass Bet is the space bar just above the "Pass Line" on the bottom and side panels on the wings. A bet on this space is almost the opposite of one placed on the Pass Line. On the "Come Out Roll" (first roll) with a bet on the Don't Pass space, the 7 or 11 loses and the 2 and 3 win but not the 12. The 12 is a tie in this case and no one wins or loses. Pay-off on this space is one-for-one.

The "Field Bet" space is the third space up from the bottom of the wing. It contains the numbers 2, 3, 4, 9, 10, 11, and 12 with the numbers 2 and 12 circled and the message near both of them saying "Pays Double." If you want to bet the Field because it looks like such a good bet, you would put your bet on Field just before the next throw of the dice. If any one of those seven numbers in the Field space came up you would win one-for-one on your bet; if 2 or 12 came up you would be paid twice your bet. If none of those numbers came up on that throw of the dice, you would have lost your bet.

In the center section, or body of the bird, are an array of bets that pay off in big odds as each panel states. Since the stickman controls the center section, bets are tossed to the center of the section by the player, who calls to the stickman to tell him the bet. As an example: "Five dollars, twelve." With his stick, the stickman pushes your bet onto the panel that shows the two sixes and states that it pays 30 for 1. If 12 comes up on the next roll, the stickman will push your winnings in front of you but leave your original bet on the two sixes panel; it will remain there awaiting the next roll of the dice unless you tell him to "take down" your wager and return it to you.

Now look at the rest of the craps table. Two sections called "Big 6" and "Big 8" on the bottom corner of the wings block the Don't Pass as it turns to the top of the wings. These "Big" numbers really don't have any special meaning because a bet on either one of them just pays off one-for-one. A bet on either one is a winner if the number bet comes up before a 7 but is a loser if the 7 comes up first.

There are many other ways to play craps, but they are more applicable to professional gambling operations than to casual players at a fundraiser, so they will not be described here.

It is difficult to estimate the probable income of this game because there are so many ways the game can be played. However, if the rules are kept simple, any fundraiser can realize a good profit on a craps table and it will be fun at the same time.

Craps has been played both indoors and out. Any place where a group of people can circle around a patch of space and roll those ivories is suitable. The craps tables in casinos are ornate, bulky, and heavy — certainly not suited for portability. Your organization needs something simple to make and easy to move and store, while being reliably functional.

BUILDING INSTRUCTIONS FOR THE CRAPS TABLE (FIGURE 13)

Materials Needed		
Plywood		
2	4' x 8'(¼")	
Lumber		
7	1" x 2" x 8'	
Dowels, wooden		
2	⅜" x 36"	
Screws (for wood)		
2 lbs.	¾" #6	
16	2½" x #8	
Nails (finish)		
1 lb	#10d	
Paint		
Foam sheets and felt (optional)		

Creating the Frame:

1 Cut four 1 x 2 x 8's to 93 inches (These will be the long sides). Cut another two 1 x 2 x 8's into four 48" pieces. (These will be the short sides.) Cut one 1 x 2 x 8 into ten 5" pieces. (These will be the braces.)

2 Lay two 93-inch pieces on a flat surface, with the 2-in. side facing up. Place the two 5-in. pieces (with the 2-inch side facing up) between them at each end; nail together with finish nails. Place the third 5-in. piece in the center and nail it. (See Figure 13, side view.) Repeat for the other long side.

3 Take four 48-in. pieces and four 5-in. pieces and, in a similar manner, construct the short sides. Nail together with finishing nails.

4 Create a box with the four sides, using 2½ #8 wood screws in each corner. This is the frame.

5 Screw one of the pieces of plywood to the frame with the ¾-in. #6 wood screws, placing one screw every 4 in. around the perimeter.

6 Cut two 12" x 93" and two 12" x 45½" pieces out of the second sheet of plywood. With wood screws, affix these pieces to the inside of the box, starting with the long sides.

Finishing the Table:

1 Paint the entire table, using at least two coats of paint.

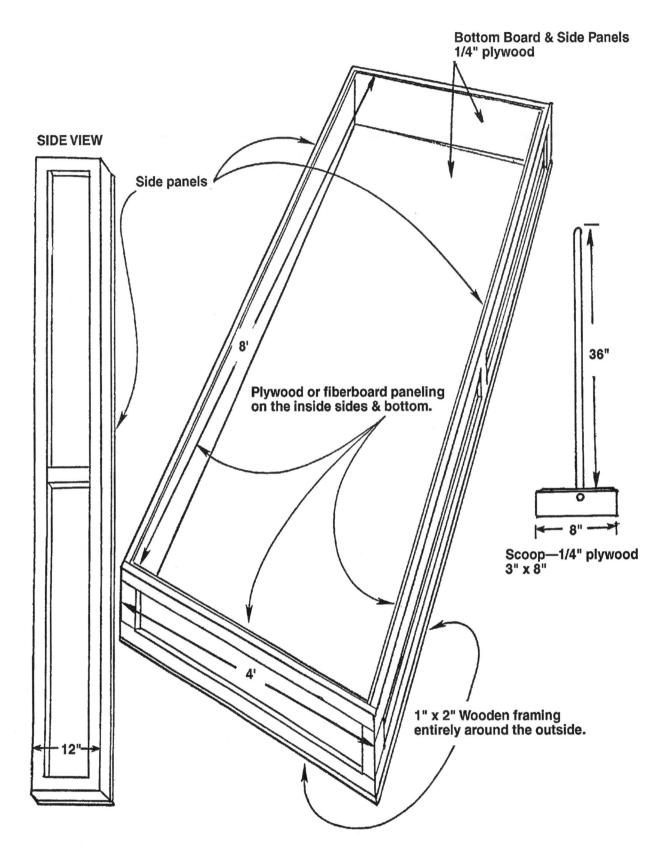

Bottom Board & Side Panels
1/4" plywood

SIDE VIEW

Side panels

8'

Plywood or fiberboard paneling
on the inside sides & bottom.

36"

8"

Scoop—1/4" plywood
3" x 8"

4'

1" x 2" Wooden framing
entirely around the outside.

12"

Figure 13. Craps Table Construction

2 For a more professional look, pad the table by gluing on the foam and felt. Although this is not essential, cushioning the inside of the table with foam helps to deflect the dice as they strike the sides of the table.

3 Paint or use plastic letters to finish the table.

Making the Scoop:

1 Cut two 3" x 8" pieces of plywood. Drill a ³/₈-in. hole in each piece and glue a dowel in each of the holes.
   The craps table can be set on any sturdy surface.

HORSE RACE ROMP

How It's Played:

Maybe you can't hear the clatter of the horses' hooves, but the rattle and bang of those six cubes as they are thrown out of the container could pass as a pretty good substitute. Horse race games come in many forms and sizes. Most of them come in box-size form or as a wheel with pictures of horses painted on it. A few are individual replicas of galloping horses on a race track that takes up part of the floor in a hall or a tract of ground at an outdoor carnival. With this game of Horse Race Romp as illustrated and explained in this chapter, the illusion of a real horse race becomes more believable. The game can be run by a minimum of two people, one handling the cubes and calling out the number of spaces to advance each individual horse on the race track, and the other actually moving the horses forward on the track as directed by the announcer. Every move takes time, and it will go smoother and faster if more people are involved.

There are a number of ways this game can be run and bets made. The race track does not have to be just a sheet of plywood, but can be a much longer course with many more spaces blocked out. If it's on the ground or in a grassy area, the lines can be set down with any white powder or dust (such as white flour), and if it

is on an interior floor, masking or other tape can be used without damaging the floor.

The betting slips can be cards or paper of six different colors, one for each horse, and folded or perforated in the middle so that one half is sold to the player and the other half retained by the operators of the game. All these cardboard or paper slips should be numbered, with the same number on each end of the slip.

An easier method is simply to buy rolls of double tickets in different colors that already are numbered properly. The tickets should be sold with plenty of time before the race; be sure to have plenty of salespersons mingling in the crowds who periodically report back to the people doing the recording and calculating so they can post the ever-changing odds on each horse (determined by how many tickets are sold for each horse). The odds are easily determined by using a calculator. Here's an example: It's 7:00 P.M. and the salespeople have brought in their first reports. This is how they tally up: #1 Horse = 8 Bets; #2 Horse = 5 Bets; #3 Horse= 3 Bets; #4 Horse = 7 Bets; # 5 Horse = 11 Bets; #6 Horse = 3 Bets. Let's say the tickets are being sold for $1.00 each. That means that the salespeople have sold $37.00 in tickets so far. Working on the premise that 50% of what is collected will be set aside for prizes and the other half stays with the house, the odds would be listed as follows: Splitting $37.00 exactly would be too close to figure at this early stage, so the sum of $36.00 is used. Of this, $18 would be allocated to prizes if no more tickets are sold. To figure the odds on each horse, divide the number of tickets sold on that horse into the total allocated for prizes. For example, the odds on #1 Horse would be $18 divided by 8, or 2 1/4 to 1, or $2.25 to win. The odds on each additional horse would be as follows:

#2 Horse: 3 2/3 to 1 — pays $3.60 to win.
#3 Horse: 6 to 1 — pays $6.00 to win.
#4 Horse: 2 1/2 to 1 — pays $2.50 to win.

#5 Horse: 1 2/3 to 1 — pays $1.60 to win.

#6 Horse: 6 to 1 — pays $6.00 to win. (Some odds are rounded off for convenience. Since these are just temporary figures, if any odd figures jump out, always favor the house in rounding off.)

Back to the example. The time is now 7:30 P.M. and the salespeople have just turned in their second report. Now it's #1 Horse = 14 bets; #2 Horse= 12 bets; #3 Horse = 10 bets; #4 Horse = 11 bets; #5 Horse = 15 bets; #6 Horse = 8 bets. That brings it to a total of 70 bets or $70.00. Half of that comes to $35.00. This is how the odds change:

#1 Horse: 2 3/4 to 1 — pays $2.75 to win.
#2 Horse: 3 to 1 — pays $3.00 to win.
#3 Horse: 3 1/2 to 1 — pays $3.50 to win.
#4 Horse: 3 to — pays $3.00 to win.
#5 Horse: 2 1/3 to 1 — pays $2.30 to win.
#6 Horse: 4 1/3 to 1 — pays $4.30 to win.

Another half hour goes by, the busy salespeople are bringing in their final figures, and it's almost post time! Here are the odds as the betting closes: #1 horse = 25 bets; #2 Horse = 18 bets; #3 Horse = 22 bets; #4 Horse = 20 bets; #5 Horse = 21 bets; #6 Horse = 19 bets. That adds up to 125 bets or $125.00. Half of that is $62.50 and, rounding it down to the nearest whole dollar (favoring the house as usual), the payout total is $62.00. The final odds posted are as follows:

#1 Horse: 2 1/2 to 1 — pays $2.50 to win.
#2 Horse: 3 1/2 to 1 — pays $3.50 to win.
#3 Horse: 2 3/4 to 1 — pays $2.75 to win.
#4 Horse: 3 to 1 — pays $3.00 to win.
#5 Horse: 2 9/10 to 1 — pays $2.90 to win.
#6 Horse: 4 3/4 to 1 — pays $4.75 to win.

For one hour's work the "house" will have grossed around $65. Keeping up that same pace, they could run four races in an evening and gross around $260. The object of the game is to see which of the six horses with their jockeys goes over the finish line first to win. As shown in the illustration (Fig. 18), the cubes being thrown are not dice but blocks resembling dice, each with a large number on each of its surfaces and each side being of the same color as its horse and the number of the horse. On each face of these cubes, the right-hand corner is painted a contrasting color with a small number from 1 to 6. This indicates the number of spaces that particular colored and numbered horse should advance on the race track.

The race starts with the six horses and jockeys being on the start line as the "announcer" shakes the container holding the six cubes and then tosses them on the race track, shouting "They're off!" He then calls off the number of the horse and how many spaces it advances and the race is on. This game requires more personnel, more preparation, and more equipment, but somehow it all seems worthwhile when you're running it.

This is a game that is normally played indoors or onboard ship, but it can be played outdoors as well for a rousing good time. It is not a true dice game in that the cubes employed are made with special markings and not the standard spots of regular dice. It does require substantial preparation of the equipment and skilled fashioning and decoration of individual pieces. Although this game requires considerable attention to detail and more than the usual amount of basic materials, it is worth the effort because it creates a spirit of excitement and encourages plenty of audience participation.

BUILDING GUIDE FOR THE HORSE ROMP (FIGURES 14 AND 15)

Materials Needed
Plywood
    2   4' x 8' (½")
Upholstery foam rubber
    1 piece   2" x 4" x 6"
Dowels
    2   ½" x 3'
Wood screws
    6   2" x #8
    12   1" x #6

> Paint
>   6   Bright colors
> Dice shaker (coffee can or clean gallon paint
>   can)

Creating the Track:

1 Using one piece of plywood, create a half
   circle at one of the ends (for the track). To
   accomplish this, measure 2 ft down from one
   side and 2 ft in from another side. Where the
   two lines intersect is the center of the half
   circle. (See *Big Six Wheel, pp. 9-12,* for instructions on how to create a circle.) Cut out the
   half circle using a jig saw.
2 Sand the edges of the track and paint with at
   least two coats of base paint.
3 Paint "start" and "finish" lines (in a contrasting color). Paint in the other 16 lines as
   shown. There should be a total of 16 spaces
   on the track.

Creating the Dice:

1 Cut the upholstery foam rubber into six
   2-inch cubes.
2 Paint each one a different color. This will
   match the colors and numbers of the horse/
   jockeys that will be constructed later. Note
   that each cube has the same large number in
   the center and on every side and two smaller
   numbers in the corners in a contrasting
   color, numbered 1–6, on respective sides.
   (The small numbers indicate how many
   spaces the horse will advance on each
   throw.)

Creating the Horse/Jockey Figures:

1 Cut six 2-ft square pieces of plywood in the
   shape of the horse/jockey figures (see Figure
   15). Do this by enlarging the grid and
   sketching out each figure onto the plywood.
   Cut out with a jig saw. Paint as shown,
   using the same colors as the cubes.
2 Cut six 8-inch squares for the bases.
3 Cut the dowels into six 12-inch lengths.
   Attach the dowel perpendicular to the center
   of the base using one 2-inch screw each. Lay

the horse/jockey figure at the edge of your
work surface, locate the center of each
figure, and attach each of the base/dowel
assembly units using two 1-in. screws
each.

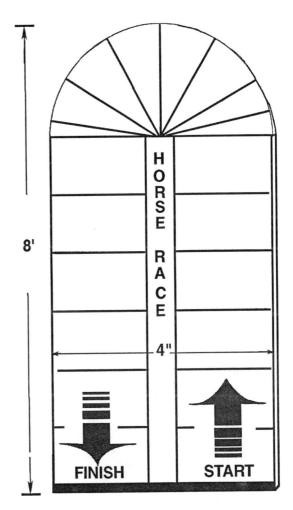

Figure 14. Horse Race Romp

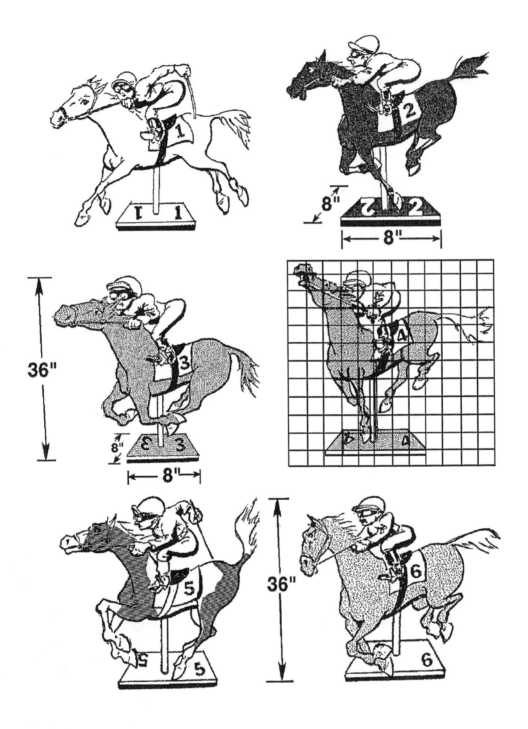

Figure 15. Horse Race Rome

UNDER AND OVER 7

How It's Played:

Looking at this game, with just three spaces to bet on (see Fig. 16), it seems like a cinch to win. At least, that's the reaction of most people when they first see this simple game. With that kind of appeal, and knowing the actual odds against the players (figured by professional gamblers at almost 17 cents on every dollar played), this game is a great money-maker for any fundraising effort.

It is a simple game to play and to operate. The players place their bets on any one of the three spaces and the operator shakes the container and tosses out the two dice. If the total sum is under seven, the bettors on the first space are winners and those on the other two spaces are losers. If the thrown sum is over seven, the last space wins and the other two spaces lose. Each time, the winning players are paid one-for-one. Finally, if the thrown sum comes out a seven, those bettors on that center space would be paid four-for-one. This is an excellent game to include in any event because it is easily portable and requires little space for playing, storage and operation. It can be operated by one person.

BUILDING GUIDE FOR UNDER AND OVER 7
(FIGURE 16)

Materials Needed

Plywood
       1   4' x 8' (½")
Upholstery foam rubber (optional)
       1 piece   2" x 2" x 4"
Paint

Creating the Game Table:

1 This is one of the easiest games to build because it consists of only a single board. The length and width can vary, but a board cut to 2 x 6 has proven to be most satisfactory.

2 Sand and paint with two coats of paint. Add markings and numbers as shown in the figure, using bright, contrasting colors. Set it on a sturdy table.

3 Regular-sized or oversized dice can be used. The dice can be thrown by hand or from a container (such as a clean coffee or paint can). If oversized dice are to be used, cut two 2-inch cubes from the upholstery foam rubber and paint like standard dice. Any reasonable number of players can be accommodated.

Figure 16. Over and Under 7

CHUCK-A-LUCK GAME

How It's Played:

The original chuck-a-luck was originally often called "bird cage" because of the hourglass-shaped cage used for shaking the three dice before releasing them on the betting table. Rather than try to duplicate the "cage," if it is not available to rent or purchase, a different device has been worked out that performs the basic principles of the game without the standard cage. In this new version, the three dice are placed on a shelf divided into three sections, one for each of the dice, and there is an extending handle that will be lifted, either by the operator or a player, to allow the three dice to tumble down a sloping board through a coned cage, deflected by angled bits of wood attached to the sloping board, onto a fenced area where they come to rest. The betting board is at the front of the game base.

Some operators may question the feasibility of including this game in their stock of games since the "take" is figured at a meager return of about seven and a half cents on every dollar played. That's a private decision to make, but it's here for those who may want it.

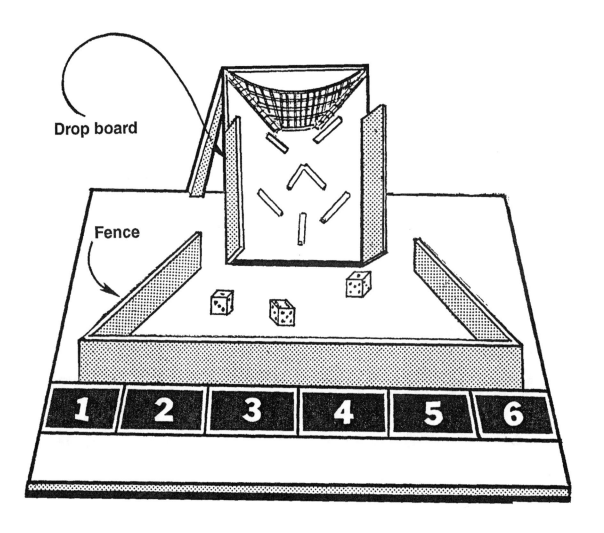

Figure 17. Chuck-a-Luck

BUILDING GUIDE FOR CHUCK-A-LUCK
(FIGURE 17)

Materials Needed

Plywood
    1   4' x 8' (½")
Wire mesh
    1 piece   12" x 30" (½")
Screws (wood)
    1 box   ¾" x #8
Upholstery foam rubber
    1 piece   2" x 2" x 6"
White glue

Creating the Fence:

1 Cut the plywood sheet into the following
   pieces: one 4' x 4' (for the base), one 24" x 12"
   (for the drop board), two 4" x 18" (for the
   drop board deflectors), seven ½" x 2" (tumblers), two 2" x 24" (for supports), two 4" x
   24" (short side of the fence) and one
   4" x 40" (for the long side of the fence).

2 All of the wood should be sanded and
   painted with two coats of paint, paying
   special attention to the edges. With a contrasting color, paint the numbers 1 through 6
   on the front edge of the base.

3 With wood screws, attach the 4 x 40 fence
   from the underside of the base. The fence
   should be mounted so that it is parallel to
   the front, but behind the numbers, and 4
   inches from each side.

4 Again, with wood screws, attach the two
   4 x 24 pieces to the base so that they meet at
   the edges of the front fence and angle back
   so the rear edges are 16 inches from the side.

Creating the Drop Board:

1 The drop board is constructed from the
   24 x 12 piece of plywood with the two 4 x 18
   deflectors screwed into the side. Screw the
   top of the wire mesh to the drop board to
   form a cone shape. Be sure that the wire
   mesh is attached so that the bottom opening
   is large enough for one of your "cubes" to fall
   through without getting caught and the top
   of the wire mesh projects out six or more
   inches from the drop board.

2 The seven tumblers should be attached from
   the rear with wood screws, similarly to those
   shown in Figure 17. With wood screws,
   attach the two 2 x 18 supports to the back
   of the drop board at a 60° angle (approximately). The dropboard can be perma-
   nently attached to the base with screws if
   desired. Place the entire unit on a sturdy
   table.

Creating the Dice:

1 Cut the upholstery foam rubber into three 2
   x 2 cubes. Paint to resemble dice.

CHAPTER 4

▼

CARD GAMES

Some games create a constant din of noise and boisterous reaction. Not so with card games, which, although charged with high excitement and anticipation, evoke little outward expression. The "poker face" seems to be a tradition in the world of card games. Two popular card games will be described in this chapter: blackjack and poker.

A reminder: in both blackjack and poker, be sure to use the "straight" deck of cards, not a pinochle deck.

BLACKJACK

Blackjack is a simple card game that has been around a long time. No special knowledge of the game is required in order to operate it successfully; as with other games intended for a temporary setup such as a fair or carnival, the idea is to have fun and to draw players in, so the betting and playing procedures will be described in simplified form. For instance, the dealer will establish betting limits in the game, and the money that is used for betting will most likely be "funny money." There may also be a fee paid to the house by each player on every hand. Most of the other rules governing the game of blackjack remain the same.

Each player, plus the dealer, are dealt one card at a time, each of which has a particular

value. An ace can be counted either as 1 or 11. All face cards are counted as 10. Numbered cards have their actual face value. To win the game, a player must have a hand better than the dealer, meaning total points as close to 21, or "Blackjack," without "busting" (having cards adding up to more than 21 points). Having the combination of a face card with an ace is considered a blackjack, or an automatic 21, even though, technically, it could also be counted as 11.

The blackjack board, as illustrated in Figure 18, allows for up to seven players. Play begins when the dealer deals one card to everyone, including himself, face down. Then he deals another card to everyone — face down to each of the players, but face up to himself. The players look at the two cards dealt to them without revealing them and decide whether to draw another card or not, based upon the value of the dealer's face-up card. If a player feels the dealer holds a better hand than himself, he will call for another card. If he feels he holds a better hand than the dealer can draw, he will not call for any more cards. (If he is dealt a blackjack — an ace and a face card or a 10 — he will lay his two cards face up and wait for the dealer to come to him after he, the dealer, shows his final hand to the players.)

After the dealer has dealt the first two cards to the players and to himself, he will turn to the last player to his left, who will say "hit" if he wants another card, or, as they do in casinos, scrape the tip of his cards on the table toward himself, indicating that he wants a card. If the player doesn't want any more cards, he will say "enough" or place his hand above his cards and shake his head.

When a player "busts" by calling for cards until the sum is over 21 points, the player will lay his cards on the board face up, indicating he has lost. After the dealer has completed dealing to everyone, he turns up his own face-down card to reveal what he has. If the sum is less than 17 he will deal a card from the deck until he has 17 or over. If he deals himself a bust he will pay off all the players who do not have a bust. If he stops with a sum of 17 to 21, he will pay those players whose cards total more than his, collect the bets of the players who have less than he has, and collect the bets of the ones who have busted.

If a player has the same sum as the dealer it is considered a "standoff" and no one wins or loses; the bet remains where it was put, or the player may decide either to remove it or increase it. This completes that particular play. To begin the next round, the players place their bets in the space indicated in front of them.

If the dealer shows an ace face-up, he may ask the players if they want "insurance." This means that a player, agreeing to insurance, can bet up to half of his bet that the dealer holds a blackjack. If the dealer does have a blackjack, the player gets paid two for one for the amount he paid for his insurance, but loses his regular bet. Players who did not get insurance just lose their regular bet. If the dealer does not have a blackjack, the game proceeds as usual with only those taking insurance losing the amount they paid for the insurance.

BUILDING GUIDE FOR BLACKJACK TABLE (FIGURE 18)
This game consists of a large betting board which can be placed flat on any sturdy table. For blackjack, a chip/change box (instructions provided below) will work better than a change apron worn by the operator.

Materials Needed	
Plywood	
1	4' x 8' (½")
Lattice	
1 piece	1" x 8' (¼")
Brads	
1 package	1"
Posterboard	
1 sheet	2 x 4
Paint	

Creating the Table:

1 Mark one end of the sheet of plywood 2 ft from the edge. From this mark create a half-circle (see *Big Six Wheel, pp. 9-12*, for instructions on how to make a circle). Cut the half-circle out of the plywood sheet with a jig saw.

2 Sand and paint with at least two coats of paint. Stencil or freehand paint the lettering as shown in Figure 18.

3 Outline and paint the seven betting squares (equally spaced around the table).

Creating the Chip/Change Box:

1 From the remaining plywood, cut one 6" x 8" piece. (This will be the bottom of the chip/change box.)

2 Cut the lattice into the following: two 8-in. pieces and nine 5¾-in. pieces.

3 Cut the poster board into a 5¾" x 10" strip.

4 With the brads, nail the nine 5¾-in pieces in between the two 8-in. pieces. (This will create a lattice box.)

5 Nail the plywood to the bottom of the lattice box. Form the posterboard strip into the spaces between the lattice (forming 8 half-cylinders) and glue into position.

BLACKJACK TABLE

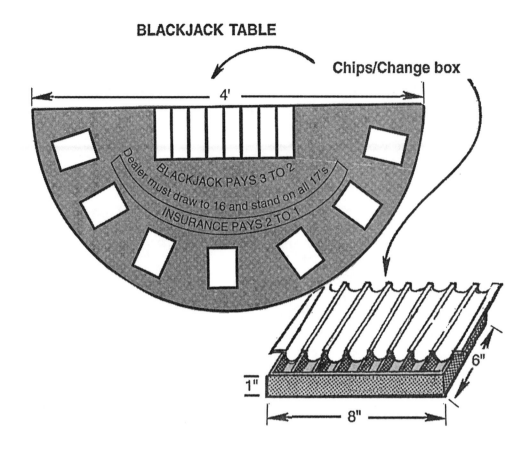

POKER TABLE TOP

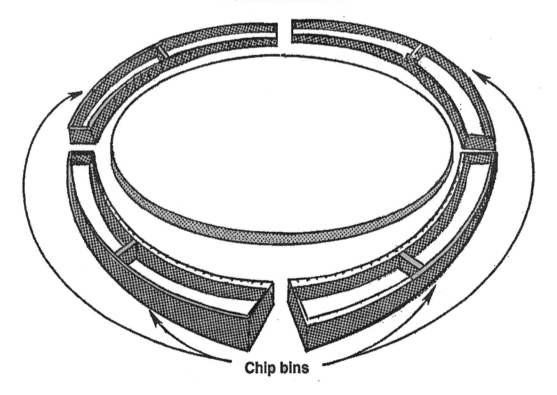

Figure 18. Blackjack and Poker Tables.

POKER

Even people who don't understand poker and have no desire to do so are familiar with the usual expressions of this game and their general meaning. But the game has many variations, some of which are well known and others undocumented. In this section we will cover the basics of the game as it is best played in fundraising situations, and offer a taste of some of the more interesting variations.

How It's Played:

In "legitimate" poker, a hand is either five or seven cards, and usually four to seven players play at one time. Players take turns betting according to the strength of their hand and the relative strength or weakness that they deduce the other players' hands to have. When everyone has "checked," meaning that they are not betting any more, each player is expected to expose his hand to the others. Most likely, but not automatically, the rules state that "the best hand on the table wins."

If there are no "wild" cards allowed (see explanation of wild cards, this page), the following rules apply for deciding which hand is the best, starting with the hand of least value:

One Pair. Two cards of the same value, such as two jacks or two deuces. (If no player's hand has even one pair, then the player with the highest single card wins. If two players each have one ace, the ace of spades would be considered higher than the ace of hearts, the hearts higher than the ace of diamonds, and the ace of clubs would be lowest in value.)
Two Pair. Two cards of the same value and two other cards of a different value, such as two queens and two fours.
Three of a Kind. Three cards of the same value, such as three queens or three eights.
Straight. Five cards in numerical or face card sequence, such as the eight, nine, ten, jack, and queen of different suits.
Flush. Five cards in the same suit, such as five spades or five hearts. They do not have to be in any particular sequence.

Full House. Three cards of the same value along with two cards of the same value, such as three kings and two tens.
Four of a Kind. Four cards of the same value, such as four sevens.
Straight Flush. Five cards in sequence in the same suit, not including the ace, such as the five, six, seven, eight, and nine of hearts.
Royal Flush. A straight flush that does include the ace (that is, ten, jack, queen, king, and ace of the same suit). If there are no "wild cards" allowed, the royal flush is the highest possible combination of cards.

Designating *"wild cards"* is a fairly common practice in private poker games, but less so in casinos. If all players agree to allow wild cards, the dealer of each game may designate which card will be "wild"— meaning that the card chosen can be used by each player for whatever card he or she wishes. In this type of play, the highest combination of cards would no longer be a royal flush, but would be five aces.

TYPES OF POKER GAMES

Stud Poker. This is one of the better known games, again for four to seven players. Either five or seven cards are dealt for each player's hand; the five-card version will be reviewed here. The dealer shuffles the deck of cards and has one of the players cut the deck. The dealer then deals a single card face down to each of the players, starting from his left. He also deals himself a card, face down. Then he deals each player and himself one card face up. He identifies the highest exposed card and invites that player to start the betting.

Often, depending on the rules of the game and general practice in the area, the game starts with a "kitty," meaning that each player places a predetermined amount of money or chips in the "pot" at the center of the table to make the prize more valuable. In nonprofessional games for fundraising, the rules may call for the "house" to take a piece of the pot at the end of each game, or for each player to pay the house a fee to enter the game.

The player who begins the betting has the option to bet up to the house limits (set by the operator); or he can "fold" (drop out) by turning his open card over. If he folds, the dealer invites the player having the next-highest card to bet. If this player bets, all the other players make the same bet to stay in the game, or they can "raise" by throwing in the amount of the original bet plus more, up to the preset limits of the house. The players following the raiser must throw in equal amounts or fold, and the players before the raiser must either fold or throw in the difference between their original bet and the raise.

The dealer repeats the same procedure for each round he deals out (all remaining cards are dealt face up) until he comes to the fifth card to be dealt. He then says "last card coming up" and deals out to the remaining players who have not folded. After the last card is dealt, the dealer again indicates the player with the best hand showing to start the betting. The player either says "check" or bets. If he checks, the rest of the players also check, all players' hands are shown, and the player with the best hand wins the pot. If the player with the best hand showing at the last card dealt bets, the other players must follow with the same amount or, if one or more of the others raise, the rest of the players must keep putting in an amount equal to the raises until no one raises further. At that point, all remaining players show their hands, and the best hand wins. If in the course of raises at the end, players keep folding until only two are left playing and one of them raises the bet and the other one folds, the raiser takes the pot without being compelled to show his hand.

Draw Poker. This is the other all-time favorite poker game, and its rules are similar to those of stud poker. The difference is in the dealing of the cards and the fact that players are able to discard some of the cards they are originally dealt and call for the same number of

cards to be dealt to them from the remainder of the deck. As in the previous game, hands can consist of either five or seven cards. The five-card version will be reviewed here.

At the start of the game, the dealer deals each player and himself five cards, face down, one card at a time. Usually the dealer will announce the minimum value required to open the betting. A favorite rule is "Jacks or better to open." This means a player must have at least a pair of jacks or some better combination to start the betting. If no player can open, the hands are thrown in, shuffled, and dealt again with the same announcement. This time the opener throws in his bet and discards the cards from his hand that he does not want. The other players who wish to stay in the game do the same and the game continues. As in stud poker, the players may start by putting so much into a kitty to "sweeten" the pot and understand that the house gets its cut from every game played.

After each player has discarded and received new cards from the dealer, the original opener is asked to bet. If he does not wish to bet, he shows his "openers" and then folds. The next player to his left then becomes the bettor. When he bets, the rest of the players follow suit or start to raise the bet. Rules for raising bets are the same as in stud poker.

BUILDING GUIDE FOR POKER TABLE (FIGURE 18, SEE PAGE 48).

Materials Needed		
Plywood		
1	4' x 8' (½")	
1	4' x 8' (¼")	
Brads		
¼ lb.	1"	
Paint		
Glue		

Creating the Table and Betting Rail:

1 Find the center on the piece of ½" plywood. Draw two circles one inside the other: one with a diameter of 45½-in. and the other with a diameter 48-in. (instructions for

making a circle are given in *Big Six Wheel*, *pp. 9-12*). Using a jig saw, cut out the two circles, so that you have a ring with a 48-in diameter (chip bins) and a circle with a 45½-in. diameter (the table).

2 Cut the ring into four equal sections.

3 From the ¼-in. plywood, cut the following: four 2½" x 35½", four 2½" x 37½", and twelve 2" x 2½" pieces.

4 Glue and then nail the 2½" x 35½" strips to the inside of the ring. Glue and then nail the 2½" x 37½" strips to the outside of the ring. Glue and nail the 2" x 2½" dividers to the rings: one at each end and one in the middle. Nail this assembly to the edge of the table.

5 Sand and paint the entire table with at least two coats. Place on a sturdy table for playing.

CHAPTER 5

▼

FORTUNE-TELLING GAMES

Everyone loves to be told what their future will be, and in the playful atmosphere of a carnival, a lighthearted fortune based on the luck of the draw is a real crowd-pleaser. You don't have to have any psychic powers to make up fortunes: all you need is a special deck of cards and a little imagination.

There are many variations on the fortune-telling theme. This chapter describes the following three:
Happenings
Strings Attached
Roll-A-Fortune

HAPPENINGS

This is a fortune-telling game using a specially made deck of cards developed by the author.

How It's Played:

Players draw 3 or more cards, and the operator then explains the person's fortune based on the messages and the position of each card. For instance, cards to the left of the dealer may indicate past events, and cards to the right may indicate future events. The messages on the sides of the cards indicate how the fortune may change based on the combination of cards and suits.

The best way to operate this game is to let your imagination soar and the interpretations

flow easily. Avoid any "reading" that may offend or seem negative to the player. Everyone has come to your event to have a good time, and no one needs to be unduly alarmed by some supposed message in the cards. Make your "predictions" lighthearted and positive, with a hint of adventure and excitement. Fortunes need not be overly complicated. Figure 20 shows two "fortunes" as examples, with the player drawing three cards.

BUILDING GUIDE FOR HAPPENINGS
(FIGURES 19A-D)

Materials Needed
Playing cards
    1 deck
Cardboard
    Medium-weight (for mounting the cards; preferably white on one side and a bright color on the back; use the same color for all 52 cards)
Plastic sheeting for lamination (clear, self-adhesive shelf paper – optional)

Creating the Playing Deck:
1 From the cardboard, cut out 52 identical rectangles with rounded corners. (Dimensions should be ½-in. or ¾-in. wider than the playing cards.)
2 With white side of the cardboard up, glue playing cards to the center of each rectangle.

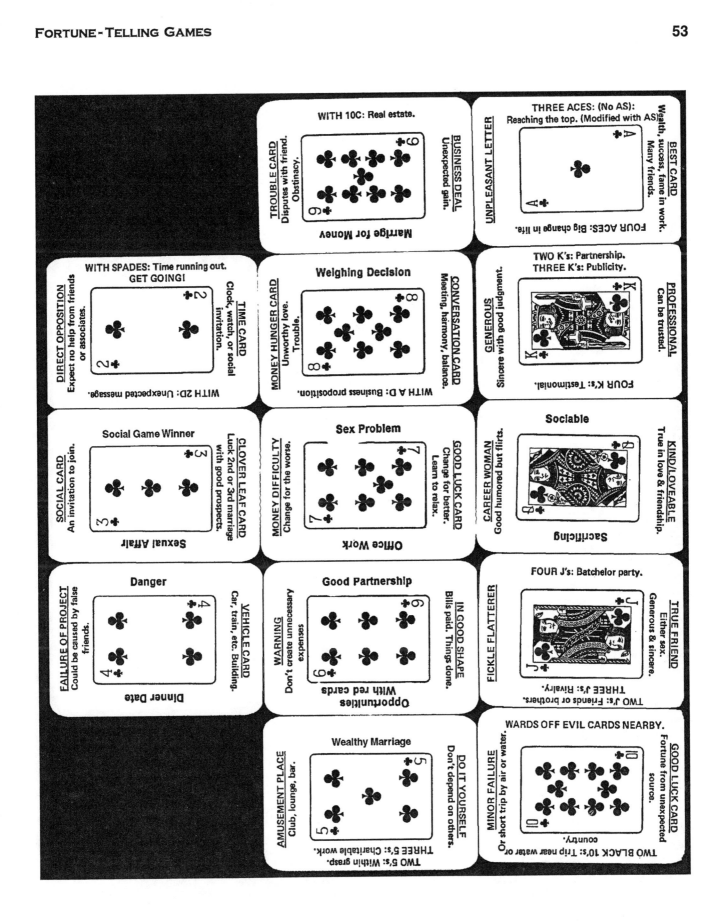

Figure 19a. Happenings Deck

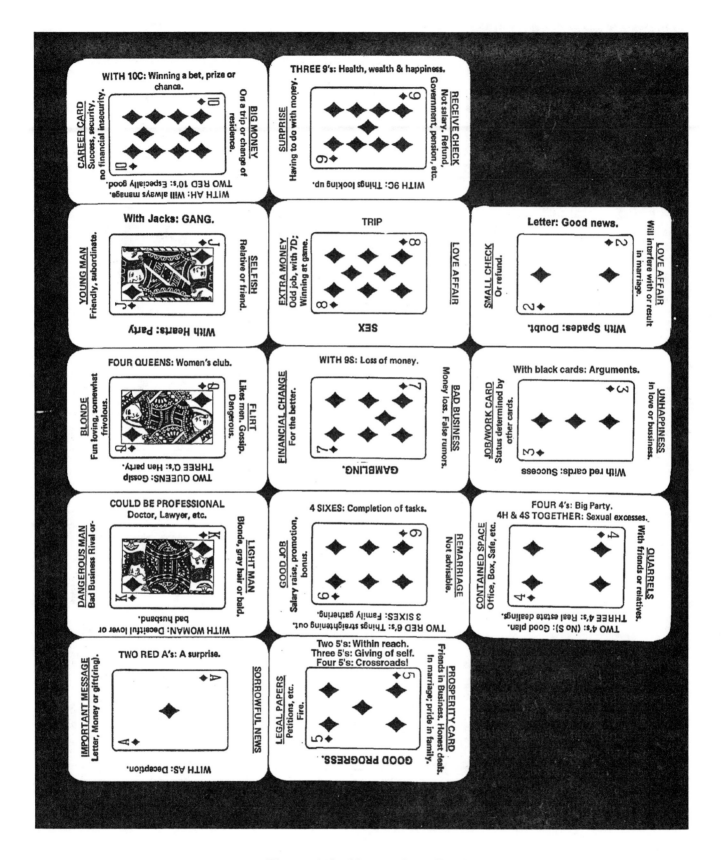

Figure 19b. Happenings Deck

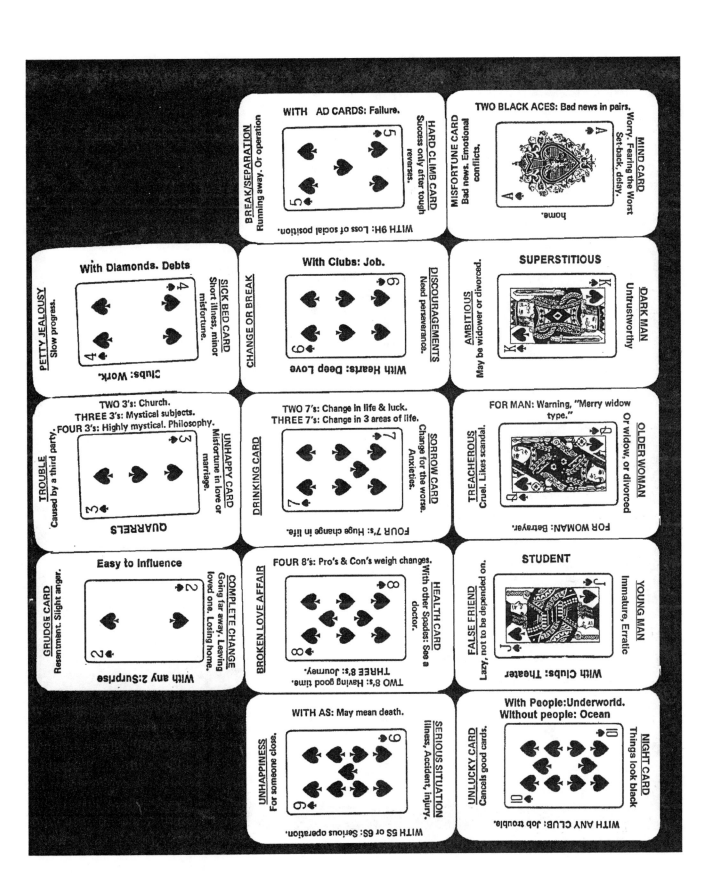

Figure 19c. Happenings Deck

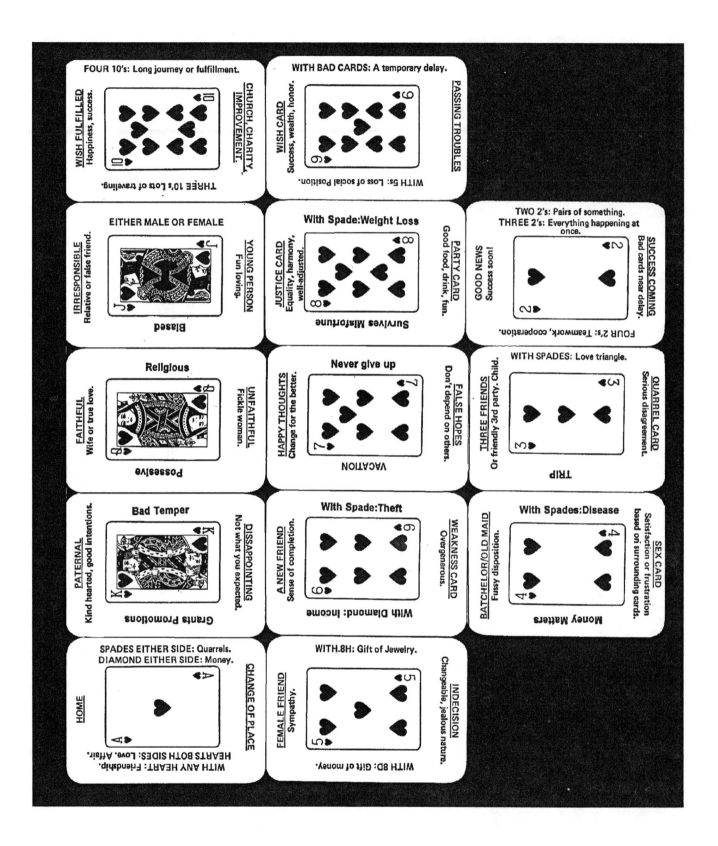

Figure 19d. Happenings Deck

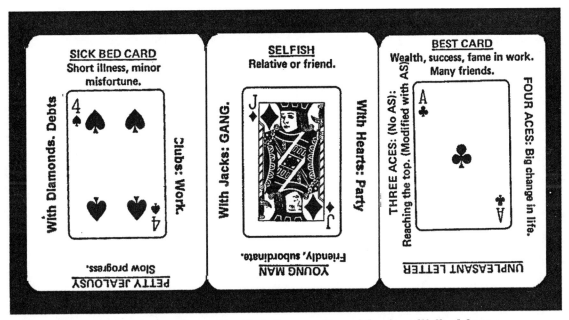

At work a young boy who wasn't doing well suddenly will find fame and success in theatrical work.

or,

Advancement at work has been slow because of a young man's foolishness but your friends help you succeed.

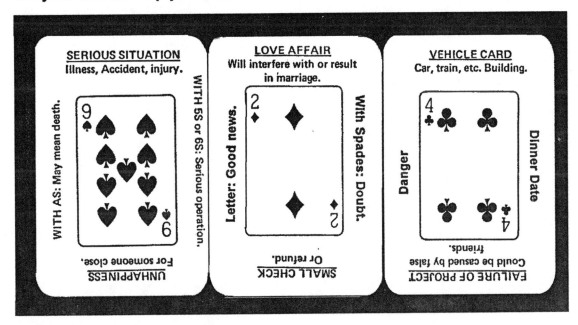

Someone has had a serious accident and marriage plans of this person are seriously affected.

or,

Although serious illness affects someone, a letter inviting them to dinner has a good effect.

Figure 20. Happenings Deck — Sample Reading

Type out fortune clues for each card, cut out, and glue around the edges of the cards. Alternatively, you can print the clues neatly directly on the cardboard.

3 For a longer-lasting deck (and to make shuffling the deck easier), laminate the cards using plastic lamination sheets or clear plastic shelf paper. (You can also get the cards professionally laminated at some print shops or office supply stores.)

For easier version, simply print or type the fortune messages directly on an ordinary deck of cards, eliminating the pasting and laminating steps needed to create an oversized deck.

STRINGS ATTACHED

This game is a variation of the String Pull Game described in Chapter 6 (*see p. 61*). In this version, the strings are attached not to specific prizes to be won, but to a "Happenings" deck of cards. Players draw three cards to determine their "fortune." Prizes can be determined by the poker combinations indicated by the drawn cards.

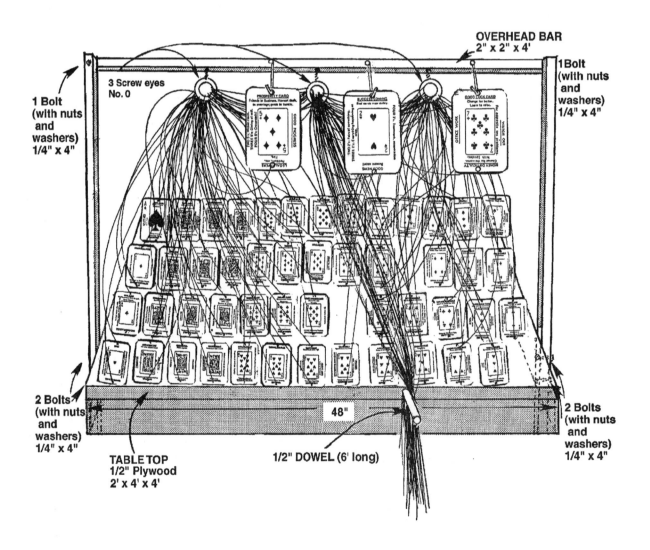

Figure 21. Strings Attached

BUILDING GUIDE FOR STRINGS ATTACHED (FIGURE 21)

Materials Needed

Plywood
    1   4' x 8' (½")
Lumber
    2   2" x 4" x 8'
    1   2" x 2" x 8'
Screw eyes
    3   #0
J-Hooks
    3   2½" #0
Dowels
    1   ½" x 36"
Machine screws/nuts
    6   ¼" x 4"
Steel washers
    12   ¼"
Nails
    8   #12d
Wood screws
    1 lb.   #8d x 1"
Playing cards (*Happenings Deck, pp. 53-56*)
String

Creating the Table:

1 Cut the 2 x 4's into two 48-in. pieces and two 45-in. pieces. Nail together to form a 4-ft square box.
2 Cut the plywood in half, creating two 4-ft squares. Take one 4-ft square and attach it to the box to form a table top. Use wood screws about every 6 inches around the perimeter.

Assembling the Game Table:

1 Cut the 2 x 2's into two 48-in. and one 51-in. piece. At the center of opposite sides of the table, attach the two 48-in pieces with machine screws, washers, and nuts. The 48-in. pieces must be perpendicular to the plywood and flush to the 2 x 4's. (Pieces will be opposite from one another.) Then attach the 51-in. piece (using machine screws, washers, and nuts) between the two uprights, creating a crosspiece.
2 Drill 3 holes equally spaced on the underside of the crosspiece and screw in the screw eyes.

3 Drill and screw in the J-hooks.
4 Drill a ½-in. hole in the front of the table just to the right of center. Glue in a 6-in. dowel.
5 Sand and paint the entire structure. Set on a table for use.

Adding the Playing Cards:

1 Make a deck of *Happenings* playing cards (*pp. 52-58*).
2 Punch two holes one on the top and one on the bottom edge of each card. Tie one end of a piece of string to the top hole and another piece of string to the bottom hole. Place the cards on the tabletop (four rows of 13 cards each) and extend the string up through one of the screw eyes and down across the dowel rod. One-third of the strings should be pulled through each screw eye.

ROLL-A-FORTUNE

How It's Played

    A large beach ball is covered with plastic sleeve-type pockets of a size into which the oversized Happenings cards can be inserted (face down) and removed easily but will hold the cards in place as the ball rolls around. Players pay a fee to the operator, roll the ball around the ring, and then pull out five cards when the ball stops rolling. The person's fortune is told, and again, prizes may be determined from the poker combinations that are pulled out by the players.

BUILDING GUIDE FOR ROLL-A-FORTUNE (FIGURE 22)

Materials required

Beach ball 22" in diameter
Plastic pockets, 52 (each large enough to hold an ordinary playing card)
Happenings deck

Building Directions:

1 Make sure the beach ball is fully inflated. Glue 52 plastic pockets all over the ball, and insert the Happenings deck made with a regular-size deck of cards (*see pp. 52-58* for instructions) face down in the pockets.

2 With ropes and stanchions (*see p. 62*, for stanchion instructions) enclose an area 10 feet in diameter. Be sure that the floor is smooth.

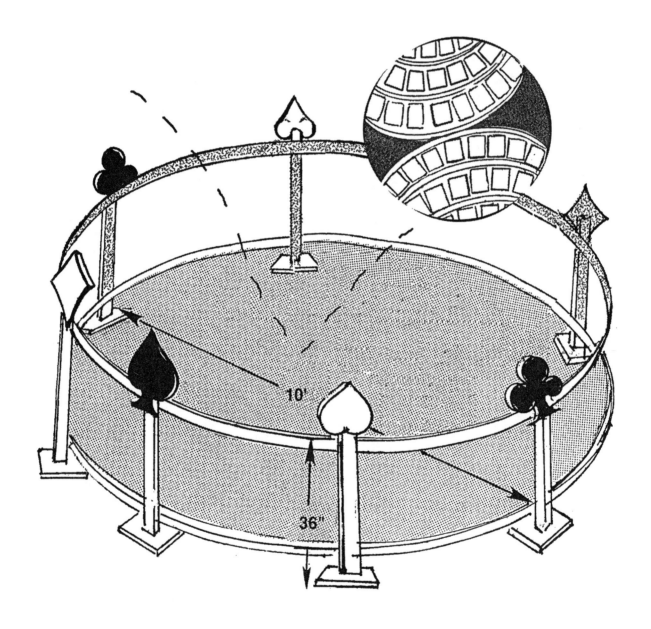

Figute 22. Roll-a-Fortune

CHAPTER 6

▼

MISCELLANEOUS
GAMES OF CHANCE

Every carnival or fair should have several games where everyone wins something just for playing. This makes the event fun for everyone; even young children can take their chances by pulling a string, tossing a penny, or reaching into a bag of prizes. In this chapter, we'll look at the String-Pull Game, Pig-in-a-Poke (also known as Grab Bag), Pitch-a-Penny, and Coin Toss.

STRING PULL GAME

How It's Played:

Whenever there are strings attached to almost anything, suspicions automatically surface. However, this bunch of strings incites only the mystery of what string to pull to get which prize. The object of the game is to pay the operator for the privilege of pulling one string in the bunch that he or she puts before you; you win whatever prize is attached to the string you select. There is no way of knowing which is the better string to pull because there are so many strings and they're completely mixed up.

It is a very simple game and can be run by one operator. Setting up this game does not require any special know-how or complicated materials, simply a table or other platform to place the prizes on, sturdy strings, and a simple frame to hold the strings.

Return of profit based upon the amount of money spent by players is somewhat hard to figure because of the different kinds of prizes that are offered that will affect the returns, but a very loose figure is about 25 cents out of every dollar.

BUILDING GUIDE FOR STRING PULL GAME

Materials needed:
See materials list for Strings Attached, *p. 59.*

Building directions
1 Build the frame and tabletop as for Strings Attached (*see p. 59*); you may also adjust the dimensions of the table and cross bar to accommodate a larger table with more prizes.
2 Attach the ends of the strings to a variety of inexpensive prizes arranged on the tabletop in a crowded array so it's impossible to tell which string goes with which prize. Have a rope and stanchions set up a few feet away from the table so players will have a more difficult time guessing which string is attached to which prize.

PIG-IN-A-POKE (GRAB-BAG)

How It's Played:

Nothing could be simpler than this game. A heavy sack or bag, opaque so its contents can't be seen, is filled with inexpensive prizes.

61

The player pays a fee to reach in the bag without looking inside and pull out something that feels interesting, which becomes his or her prize.

PITCH-A-PENNY GAME

How It's Played:

Maybe the penny is becoming obsolete to many, because it is not uncommon to see people not bothering to pick up a penny, but the Pitch-a-Penny game still survives. Even though this game and the Coin Toss (following) require some skill when actually aiming for particular squares, I've left these two games in the "Games of Chance" section because most people simply toss the coins and take their chances on how much they will win.

The object of the game is for players to pitch pennies onto the board so that they cover any of the numbered spaces without touching a line. If they succeed, the numbered value of the space is multiplied by the penny, and that amount is what they win. Any penny touching a line anywhere on the board or falling off the playing area is lost. This board usually gets a lot of play; people playing it normally exhaust all the pennies they have even when they win occasionally. Returns on this game depend heavily on the quantity of people at the affair. With a large attendance it is not unusual to pull in $15 in an hour. One operator can handle this game, and no booth is required.

BUILDING GUIDE FOR PITCH-A-PENNY (FIGURE 22)

Materials Needed
Plywood
        1   4' x 8' (½")
Paint (Black and White)
Masking tape
Numbers
Adhesive tape, thin black (optional)

Creating the Gameboard:
1 Cut the plywood in half, creating a 4-ft square.

2 Sand and paint with two coats of white paint.
3 Paint into squares with black paint (no more than 1/8-in. larger than a penny). Use masking tape to keep painting lines uniform. Alternatively, use thin, black tape to divide into squares. Refer to the figure for ideas on how to vary the board design.
4 Paint or affix numbers.

The finished board lies flat on the floor (or ground), with ropes and stanchions to keep the players about 4 ft away. Directions for building stanchions follow.

BUILDING GUIDE FOR STANCHIONS (FIGURE 22A)
(Instructions are for building four stanchions)

Materials Needed
Lumber
        1   2" x 4" x 8'
Dowels
        4   1" x 36"
Clothesline   1
Wood screws
        8   1½" x #12
        4   3" x #8

Creating the Stanchions:
1 Cut the 2 x 4 into eight 12-in. pieces.
2 Rout out the centers of each piece.
3 Fit two pieces together (this will create one base section), and screw together (two #12 screws). Continue in the same manner with the other three base units.
4 Drill a 1-in. hole in the center of the base unit (for the dowel). Insert the dowel.
5 Drill a pilot hole where the 2 x 4's intersect and through the dowel (this is to prevent the wood from splitting). Screw together using the #8 screws.
6 Drill a ½-in. hole near the top of the dowel for the clothesline.
7 Set up the stanchions spaced apart as needed, and thread together with the clothesline.

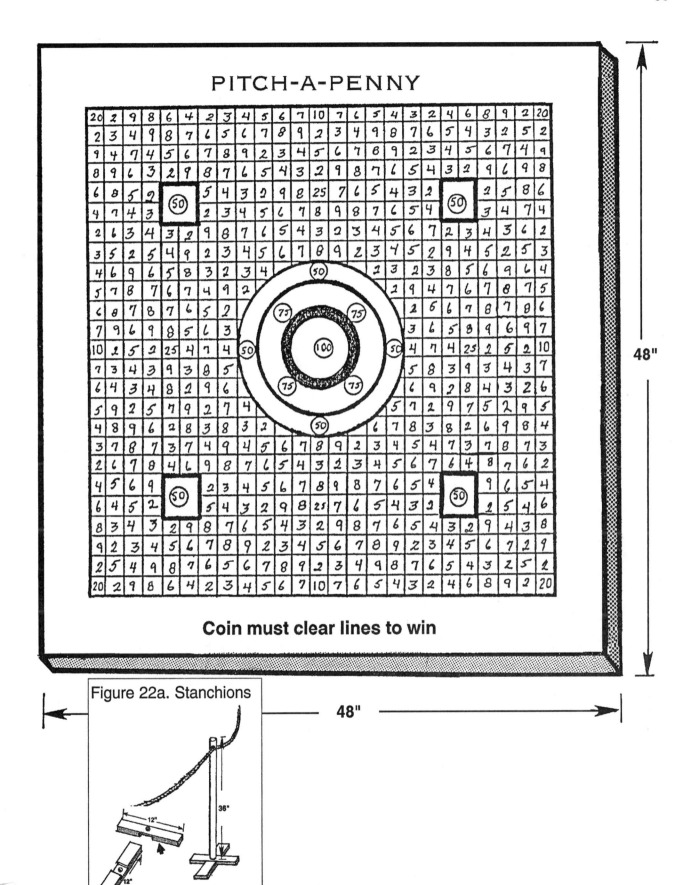

Figure 22. Pitch-a-Penny

COIN TOSS GAME

How It's Played:

This spin-off of Pitch-a-Penny brings the penny game into modern times by going from "copper" to "silver." Here, nickels, dimes, and quarters are allocated their own game boards in different corners of a larger board. Winning tosses are computed similarly to the penny game: the number painted on the square on which the coin lands is multiplied by the value of the coin. Winners can collect up to 10 times the value of the coin tossed. As in the penny game, the object of the game is to pitch the specific coin into the proper area allocated for it and have it rest in a space without it touching a line. If actual money cannot be used, chips can be substituted and points given to the winner which can be redeemed for specific prizes. The profit ratio for this game should be quite high for the "house" because it is usually quite difficult to win much on this game. It is safe to anticipate a return of 50 cents on every dollar played on this game.

BUILDING GUIDE FOR COIN TOSS GAME
(FIGURES 23A AND 23B)

Materials Needed

Plywood

| 1 | 4' x 8' (½") |

Wood screws

| 8 | 1" x #6 |

Paint (Black and White)

Adhesive tape, thin, black (optional)

Creating the Top of the Game Board:

1 Cut the plywood in half into two 4-ft squares.

2 On one of the squares, draw two diagonal lines connecting in opposite corners. Mark off 7-in. squares on opposite corners and cut out. Cut the square in half diagonally from the corners where you have cut out the 7-inch square. Measure and mark the center of one of these pieces. (This will be divider A.) Cut a ½-in. notch about one-half the distance outward toward the top corner. Take the second piece (divider B), and cut a ½ in. notch from the corner about one-half the distance inward toward the bottom (cut surface).

3 Paint and decorate as shown in the figure.

Creating the Base of the Gameboard:

1 Take the second square (the other piece of 4 x 4 plywood) and divide into quarters. Within each quarter, draw another box, leaving about a 2-in. border around each one.

2 Mark as for the Pitch-a-Penny game (*pp. 62-63*), taking care that each square is 1/8-in. larger than the coin value for that particular gameboard. For example, if the gameboard is to be for dimes, be sure that the squares are 1/8-in. larger than a dime. Note that blacked-out squares on a particular gameboard represent losing squares.

Assembling:

1 Fit the two dividers together, and mount on top of the gameboard base from the underside; screw together.

2 Set up on the floor or ground. Surround with stanchions (see *Pitch-a-Penny, pp. 62-63*, for building directions) about 4 ft away on all sides.

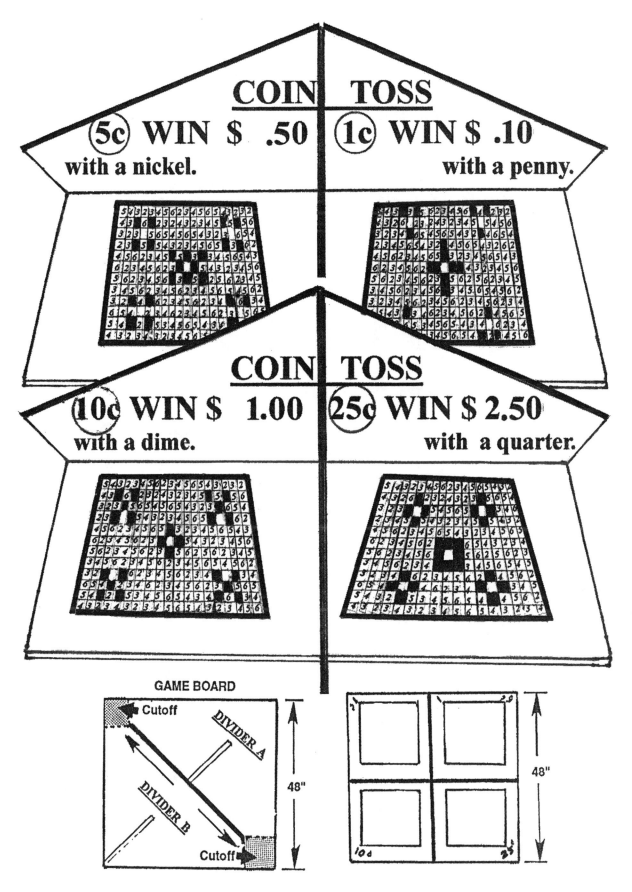

Figure 23a. Coin Toss

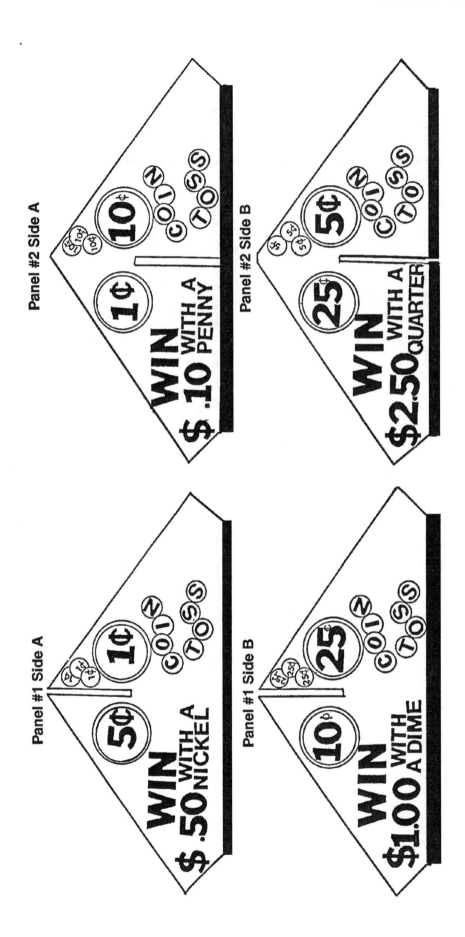

Figure 23b. Coin Toss Panels

SECTION II

GAMES *of* SKILL

Introduction

Does a cowboy get a thrill when his lasso rings a critter in the rodeo? Does a fisherman feel a sense of satisfaction when he bags a prize fish? You bet they do! And that same sense of triumph is felt by the fair-goer who successfully rings a nice watch with a hoop or throws darts at a winning card combination. Everyone loves to try their hand at hitting a target or aiming for a particular prize, and this section offers a wide selection of fun games to tempt the players.

Ball games, such as the **Bottle Game, Basketball Game, Cats on the Back Fence, and Smashin' Dishes,** allow players to hone their throwing skills as well as safely vent any frustrations! These are games that have been on the honky-tonk circuit for many years and are tried-and-true favorites.

Hoop games include variations on the theme of tossing a hoop toward a table on which various prizes have been assembled,

trying to ring the best one. They include **Ring-a-Prize, Watch-It, Peg-Leg,** and **Pitch-Till-You-Win.**

Target games use "arms and ammo" such as pop-guns, dart guns, and regular darts to hit moving or stationary targets. There is really no limit to the number of variations on target games: described here are a few favorites, such as **Wild West, Safari Game,** and **Stars and Eyeballs.**

A few games are described in Chapter 10 that are too complicated for the average person to build, but they are popular games and they are included here as suggestions for games that your organization may want to rent or purchase to make your event even more exciting.

For obvious reasons, most of these games need to be set up in a booth that is enclosed on three sides to avoid accidental "missiles" striking passers-by. (See sample booth on *pp. 4-6.)*

CHAPTER 7

▼

BALL GAMES

What kind of a fun wonderland would any fair or carnival be without those crazy games where balls are the mainstay of the operation? There would be a real void if those balls were not rolling, popping, smashing, bouncing and doing all kinds of unpredictable things all over those honky-tonk grounds.

Of all the different games that are played in fairs and carnivals, the ones in which players have to roll, toss, heave, or otherwise manipulate a ball seem to create the most action and excitement. There are so many ball games that it's hard to know where to begin. Described in this chapter are just a few of the many ball games possible:

> Bottle Game
> Basketball Game
> Cats on the Back Fence
> Smashin' Dishes
> Pit Ball Game
> Even-Up
> Roll-A-Score
> Dunk Em or Splash Em
> Camel Race

BOTTLE GAME

How It's Played:

Six identical bottles (nine for large crowds) are mounted on each of two or three stands. Each player in front of the booth throws three

baseballs at one of those stands, trying to knock those bottles off the stand. Since the "bottles" are made of wood or some other fairly weighty material, it isn't as easy as it may appear. Only one operator is needed. There should be signs in or around the booth indicating the cost of the play and what kind of prizes are being given out for winning. If the operators set up the proper distance between players and bottles, players will win a little, but not too much. The payoff on this game should average around 35 to 40 cents out of every dollar.

BUILDING GUIDE FOR BOTTLE GAME
(FIGURE 24)

Materials required
Bottles
12 to 18
Baseballs
12

Creating and Setting Up the Game:

1 Heavy wooden bottles with a wide lip may be fashioned with a lathe.
2 Alternatively, buy aluminum bottles from a game supply house.
3 Set up pyramids of bottles on sturdy stands or on shelves at the back of the booth.

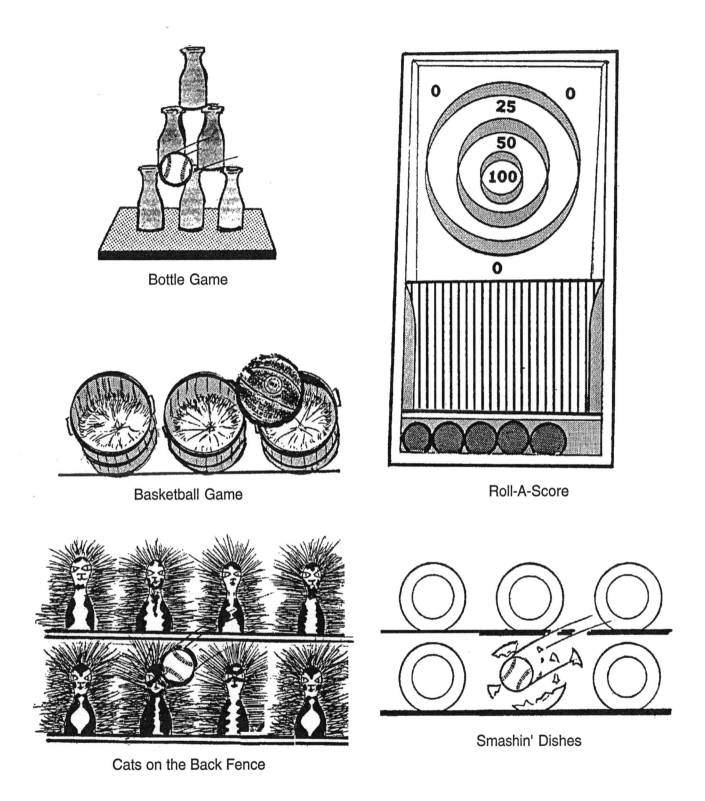

Bottle Game

Roll-A-Score

Basketball Game

Cats on the Back Fence

Smashin' Dishes

Figure 24. Assorted Ball Games

BASKETBALL GAME

How It's Played:

Players pay a fee for three throws of a basketball into bushel baskets, wooden buckets, or plastic containers. The containers are angled and the distance from the player's position to the containers is determined beforehand so that it isn't too easy to score. Basketballs or other large-sized balls can be used. The number of containers used and number of balls kept on the front stand is up to the operators, but a minimum of three baskets and three balls is recommended. If set up correctly, the profit on this game should be about 40 cents on every dollar that is played.

BUILDING GUIDE FOR BASKETBALL GAME (FIGURE 24)

Materials required
Baskets (or either wooden buckets or large plastic containers)
3
Basketballs (or beach balls)
3 standard

Creating and Setting Up the Game:

1 Tilt baskets by laying them on their side and propping the front edge up slightly with wooden blocks. Alternatively, wire the baskets to the back shelves. They can be tilted at different angles from each other to make the game even more challenging.

CATS ON THE BACK FENCE

How It's Played:

You must remember those homely, ragged "cats" sitting row on row, with long hair bristling out like a spray from the outside edge of each of them in a booth at a fair or carnival. Seems like those ugly cats have been around forever. They just seem to invite anyone to throw something at them to get rid of them. And that's what the game is all about. The player pays for three baseballs just to throw at those pesky cats and knock as many off the shelf as he or she can. But it's not so easy. Usually, there are two or three shelves with five or six cats lined up on each shelf. As the instructions will indicate, the cats are stuffed with cotton and fitted over a base made from a wooden dowel attached to a square of plywood, so a direct hit is required to knock it over, rather than a glancing blow. The way the cats are arranged on the shelves will also have an effect on the number of hits; allow enough space between each cat for a ball to pass between without touching. With careful preparation, this game should yield at least 45 cents out of every dollar played.

BUILDING GUIDE FOR CATS ON THE BACK FENCE (FIGURE 25)

Materials needed		
Plywood		
1	4' x 8' (½")	
Dowels		
2	½" x 36"	
Canvas (or Plastic cloth)		
2 yards		
Fringe (stiff)		
5 yards		
Staples		
½"		
Pillow stuffing		
Glue		

Creating the Base:

1 Cut the plywood into twelve 5-in squares (base pieces).
2 Drill a ½-inch hole in each square about ¾ in. from one side, on the center line.
3 Cut each dowel into twelve 6-inch pieces.
4 Glue dowel to each base piece.

Creating the Cats:

1 Using the enlarged pattern (*see* Figure 25), lay out on the canvas, cutting two pieces per cat. Allow ½-inch seam allowance.
2 Paint the cat features.
3 Pin fringe on the reverse side (inside) of one the pieces of canvas. Baste in place.
4 With the inside pieces facing together, sew or staple the two pieces together, leaving about 2 inches open in the bottom seam to

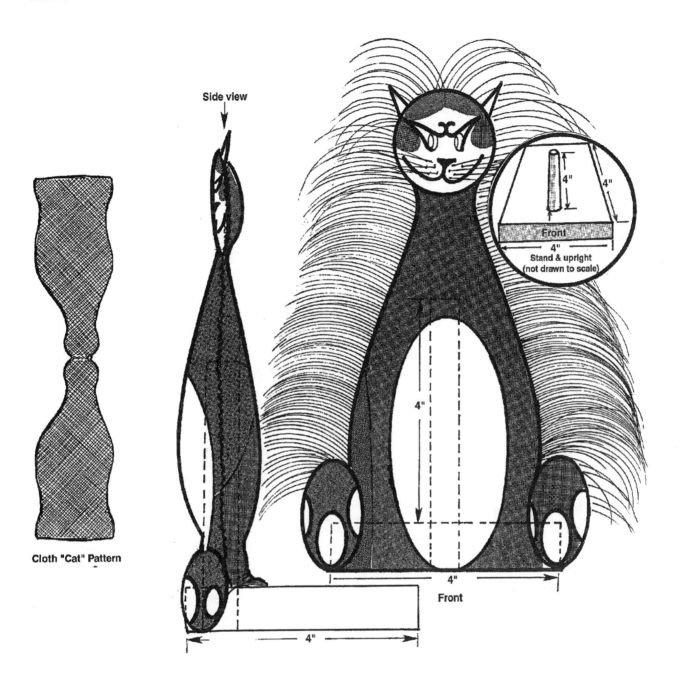

Cloth "Cat" Pattern

Figure 25. Cats on the Back Fence

allow for stuffing. Turn inside out. Stuff with pillow stuffing. Sew or staple the remaining seam, taking care to leave a ½-in. hole in the seam for the dowel.

Assembling:
1 Staple the cats over the dowel and onto each of the plywood bases.
2 Line up the cats on the shelves at the back of the booth.

SMASHIN' DISHES GAME
How It's Played:

If ever there was a game designed to provide a vent for working off stress, this should take top honors. The object for the player is to break as many dishes as possible with three throws of a baseball. The dishes should be set up on an angle and far enough apart to make it difficult for players to hit more than one plate at a time — if they hit a plate at all! Plates can also be set at different angles backward to keep the players on their toes. Dishes can be bought very cheaply at supply houses or thrift stores, so there is much less preparation and expense involved than in some of the other games. Returns on this game should run somewhat less than some of the other games because it normally doesn't draw a large crowd; a return of 35 cents for every dollar played is about average.

BUILDING GUIDE FOR SMASHIN' DISHES GAME (FIGURE 24)

Materials needed
Cheap china plates
    50   Assorted sizes and shapes
Baseballs
    12
Cardboard
    10 square feet (can use cardboard boxes)
Broom/dustpan
Receptacle for broken dishes

Building Directions
1 Cut the cardboard into 20 pieces, 6" x 12". Along the short side (6 in.), make a fold 1 inch from the edge. Make a second fold 5½ in. in from the first fold. This will form a rough "S" shape for the dish stands. (The back fold will hold the dish upright and the short fold will prevent the dish from sliding forward.)
2 Set up the plates on the stands so that a baseball can pass, without touching, between two plates.
3 Have a broom/dustpan and receptacle handy for the occasional broken dish.

PIT BALL GAME
How It's Played:

This is one of the simplest of games to understand and play. The player just tosses a beach ball or similar large ball into a pit made from a large wading pool or small swimming pool. The ball rolls around a wooden base painted and ridged with circles or panels of varied colors or numbers and comes to rest on one of them, which is then announced as the winner. The identical colors or numbers are reproduced on the betting board where the players have previously placed their bets. This game needs only one operator. The more panels on the floor of the pit, the fewer times the players will win. Depending on how the game is set up, the return on this game should range from 30 to 45 cents on every dollar played.

BUILDING GUIDE FOR PIT BALL GAME (FIGURE 26)

Materials needed
Plywood
    3   4' x 8' (½")
Lumber
    8   2" x 2" x 8'
Beach Ball
    1   20" diameter
Swimming pool rim
    1   20' diameter
Paint, assorted colors

Creating the Gaming Board
1 Sand and paint the three sheets of plywood with a base coat.
2 Mark off 2-ft squares on two sheets of the plywood sheets. Paint each 2-ft square a different color. Stencil or paint a different letter of the alphabet in each square. Be sure to use large letters.

Creating the Betting Board
1 Divide the remaining sheet of plywood into 16 equal sections. Paint each section a different color, matching the colors used on the gaming board. Stencil the same letters of the

alphabet in each section, again to match the ones on the gaming board.

Assembling the Game Board

1 Cut the 2 x 2's into 2-ft pieces. Angle cut the bottom of each piece to form two points. These are stakes.
2 Lay the two pieces of plywood on the ground, making sure that the pieces are level. Drive the stakes into the ground so they will fit around the perimeter of the plywood. (This is to keep the ball on the gaming board.)

3 Place the swimming pool rim equidistant around the plywood gaming board.
4 Place the betting board on a sturdy table.

The following four games are included here because they are easy to rent or purchase (*see Sources and Resources*) and are popular games at most carnivals. However, since they are complicated to build, instructions are not provided. Enterprising volunteers may wish to work out simpler versions to build for your fundraiser.

Figure 26. Pit Ball Game

EVEN-UP GAME

How It's Played:

Three balls are released from the top of the game board and zigzag down to the base of the board to fall into three numbered slots. If the numbers add up to an even sum, that play is considered a winner. Sometimes, instead of balls, flat discs are used that serve the same purpose as the balls. This game needs only one operator and is usually easy to operate. Surprisingly, this game usually gives a fairly good return of about 40 cents on every dollar spent (see Figure 27).

ROLL-A-SCORE GAME

How It's Played:

This game is always a favorite and an excellent money-maker. Here, players buy wooden balls similar to the old-time "duck pin" bowling balls and throw them down a short "alley" resembling a bowling alley that slants up toward circled bins that are of different diameters fitted into each other with enough room for the wooden balls thrown toward them to fly up into the air and land into one of the areas between the numbered bins or outside of them. There is a metered scoreboard on most of these games that automatically tallies the score. Prizes are determined by whatever score is reached (see Fig. 24).

DUNK-'EM OR SPLASH GAME

How It's Played:

This game has been around a while and still generates plenty of fun and profit. An area is divided into two parts: in one section, baseballs are thrown toward a target; in the other, a platform is mounted above a tank of water, and sitting on the platform is the target-victim ready to drop into the water when a player strikes the center of the target with a baseball.

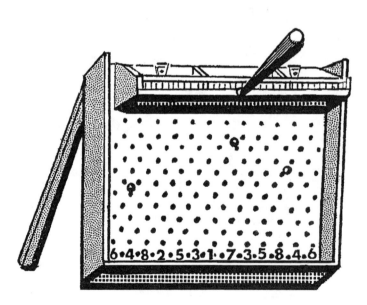

Figure 27. Even-Up Game

CAMEL RACE GAME

How It's Played:

Seen more and more at all kinds of fundraising affairs is this colorful and exciting game. In front of the large racing display where the camels march across are individual bins and a chair for each player, who is also furnished with a supply of balls. At the sound of the starting bell, each player rolls his or her balls as quickly as possible toward the openings in the bin. When a ball enters an opening, the numbered camel allocated to that player advances on the course. The game is over when one camel reaches the finish line (see Figure 28).

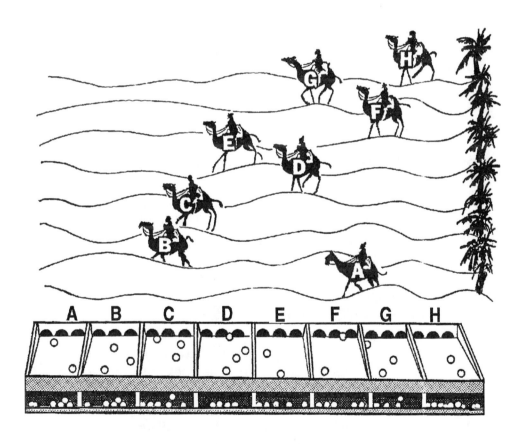

Figure 28. Camel Race Game

CHAPTER 8

▼

HOOP GAMES

"Whatever goes around, comes around!" Some of the most familiar hoop games are described in this chapter. There are many other varieties of these games, but most of them do not vary too much from the basic ones included here. Many people regard hoop games as a combination of skill and luck.

Games described in this chapter are Ring-A-Prize, Watch-It, Peg-Leg, and Pitch-Till-You-Win.

RING PRIZE OR RING-A-PRIZE

How It's Played:

This is probably one of the most popular games in this section because there are so many types of prizes that can be won. A wide assortment of prizes lend themselves to this game: Some examples are stuffed animals, decorative knickknacks, glassware, toys, and silverware. Also consider food products that come in boxes, cans, or bottles; or maybe inexpensive small appliances or electronic gadgets. Use your creativity to amass an assortment of prizes that will surely tempt the fair-goers. (To determine the number of prizes to have on hand, figure on about twice the number of items that can fit on the table with room for hoops to encircle them and fall flat to the tabletop. If you expect a very large crowd, you may wish to increase the number.)

This game can be run by a single operator and should be housed in an enclosed booth. The return on this game depends upon how the prizes are arranged and, of course, the value of the prizes being offered. If the prizes are very cheap, or if most or all of them have been donated to the organization, a very high percentage of profit will be reached. The operator should also carefully calculate the distance between the throwing line and the prize table so that there is more difficulty to winning than may first appear to passers-by.

SETTING UP THE GAME

The number of objects to be won on the table is limited only by the actual area of the tabletop. Whether the table should be flat or tilted depends on the operator. Precautions should be taken to keep the prizes reasonably rigid so that the force of the thrown hoop or some other factor won't topple the prize. This is especially important if the table is tilted. The table does not need to have a cover underneath the prizes if it has a clean, unscarred surface. Sufficient room should be allowed between the prizes to allow the hoops to fall flat to the tabletop (a condition for winning). Prizes that are more expensive should be placed so that they will be more difficult to encircle, and the least expensive ones should be relatively easy to ring with the hoop. The hoops must be large enough to encircle the prize and fall flat on the top of the table.

Some rehearsal may be necessary to determine the optimum distance between the player's position and the table holding the prizes to be most effective for controlling the profit element. Making it too easy for players to win prizes neutralizes the purpose of have a money-making game, though occasional wins are important to encourage people to try their skills at winning.

BUILDING GUIDE FOR RING-A-PRIZE (FIGURE 29)

Materials Required
Prizes
Must be of a size that will allow a uniform-sized hoop to slide over them easily and be able to land on the table around the prize in a flat position. Since there isno restriction on the type of prizes that can be used in this game outside of the hoop size factor, use either a mix of unrelated objects or a uniform type of prize, such as dolls or stuffed animals. The ideal prize has a flat bottom and is lumpy or has many angles.
Hoops
18 (approximately)

Building Directions
1 The booth should be large enough so that the prize table can be set the right distance from the front counter.

WATCH-IT GAME

How It's Played:

As opposed to having many different prizes to "catch" with a hoop toss, this game concentrates on one particular favorite prize: watches. Watches are a very popular prize and if you display many different kinds, the booth will be very popular because it looks so easy to win.

With the almost limitless variety of watches that are available through many sources, a respectable display of watches for prizes in a game of chance such as this is quite possible without laying out a great deal of money. It is even possible to obtain a supply of watches for an occasion such as your fair or carnival on a strict consignment basis.

In this game, you will need to make small pedestals for holding the watches. Although this takes time and material, the pedestals can be used over and over, stored in a relatively small space, and they are easily portable. They give the appearance of being easy to ring with a hoop, but it is actually more difficult than it appears.

As in all target games, care must be taken to place the watches correctly on the table and calculate the right distance between the players and the display to benefit the most from retaining player interest while not having them win too many prizes. Since the pedestals with the prizes will be fastened to the platform or table, some experimentation might be in order.

The prize platform can be placed flat, tilted down toward the players, or tilted down away from the players and toward the back of the booth. If you experiment with each position, you will find a marked difference in how easy is it to ring a prize with the table in different positions. Only one operator is needed. A good return is about 30 cents on the dollar.

BUILDING GUIDE FOR WATCH-IT GAME (FIGURE 29)

Materials needed
Plywood
1   4' x 8' (½")
Lumber
2   2" x 4" x 10'
Wood screws
36   2½" x #8
Carpenter's glue
Paint
Staples/rubber bands/wire
Watches
Hoops

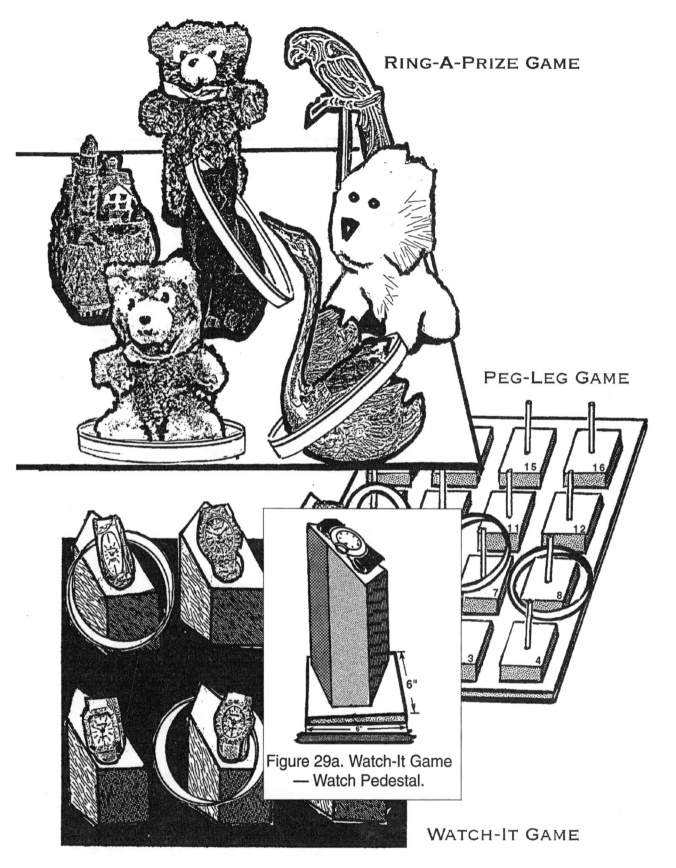

RING-A-PRIZE GAME

PEG-LEG GAME

Figure 29a. Watch-It Game
— Watch Pedestal.

WATCH-IT GAME

Figure 29. Hoop Games

Creating the Watch Pedestals:

1 Using a table or radial arm saw at a 45⁰ angle, cut down the length of each 2 x 4 from the center of one of the narrow sides. Repeat for the other side. (When viewed from the end, the 2 x 4 will now be house-shaped.)
2 Cut the 2 x 4's into thirty-six pieces of varying lengths (from 4- to 10-inch pieces). Angle cut the top edge.
3 On the sloped surface of each of the 2 x 4's, drill a 1-inch hole about ½-inch deep. (This hole will accommodate the watch.) Sand and paint a dark color.
4 Cut the plywood into 37 pieces as follows: one piece 4' x 4' and 36 pieces 6" x 6". Sand and paint a dark color.

Assembling the Game:

1 Attach each watch stand to the center of the 6-inch pieces of plywood using carpenter's glue. Allow to dry.
2 From the underside of the 4' x 4' square, attach each watch pedestal and base with wood screws. Be sure to space evenly on the plywood.
3 Place watches in the hole on each watch stand. Depending on the watch type, use staples, rubber bands, or wire to attach the watch to the pedestal
4 Set on a table for use.

Note: Throwing distance must be determined by the game operator, after a few tries. Even during the game, the operator can make an adjustment.

PEG-LEG GAME

How It's Played:

Here is a simple hoop game developed by the author that has survived competition with all the standard hoop games. Peg-leg is a rather simple product of blocks, pegs, and board that takes little time or effort to build and can be operated with ease. See the illustration in Figure 29. Each block is numbered, and a chart hung at the back of the booth indicates what

prizes correspond to which numbers. An alternate set-up is for each block to have a numbered tag at its base, and to have each prize carry a numbered tag as well.

As in other hoop games, the player buys a number of hoops for a fee or ticket, as advertised, and tosses them toward the game board, trying to circle a peg. Similar profit projections as with the other hoop games can be expected.

BUILDING GUIDE FOR PEG-LEG (FIGURE 29)

Materials needed	
Plywood	
1	4' x 8' (½")
Lumber	
2	2" x 4" x 8'
Dowels	
7	3' x ½"
Wood screws	
49	1½" x #8
Paint	
Wood hoops	

Creating the Blocks:

1 Cut the 2 x 4's into 49 blocks, approximately 3½" x 3½".
2 Drill a ½-inch hole 1-inch deep into the center of each block.

Assembling:

1 Cut the dowels into 5-inch pieces. Glue one dowel into each block.
2 Cut the plywood in half (4' x 4'). From the underside, screw each block into the square. Be sure to space evenly.
3 Sand and paint the entire assembly in contrasting colors.

Note: Hoops should be of a size just large enough to clear the blocks easily but not too much larger. Hoops can be purchased in many retail outlets or can be found in art or cloth supply stores, or even some variety stores. Mount the platform on a flat surface — or a tilted one if you want the game to be more difficult.

PITCH-TILL-YOU-WIN GAME

How It's Played:

In the three previous games, the players buy a certain number of hoops and take their chances on winning something with that number of tries. In this game, players can be sure of one thing: no matter how many hoops they have to throw, they'll finally walk away a winner of something. That's a pretty good enticement for fair-goers, since nobody likes to lose. So what if most of the prizes won are not the greatest? They are prizes, after all, and that's the way some look at it.

The profit to the house on this depends upon careful planning to find the delicate balance of how much to give to the public in prizes and still show a substantial profit. Obviously, a lot depends on the kinds of prizes being offered and how the prizes are arranged on the board. Since the object of the game is for players to throw as many hoops as possible until they win something, it is necessary to make some pegs easier to hoop than others. This can be controlled by varying the size of the pegs and how they are placed on the board. Also, the board can be flat or tilted. As in all the hoop games, testing different positions will give the most satisfactory results. Hoops should be of a size that goes over each post easily and can fall flat on the board between posts. Be sure to test the action of the hoops on the board before allocating the prize numbers to the individual posts and to deter-

mine the best distance between the playing board and the player. Inexpensive items should be those most likely to be won, whereease the more expensive and glamorous items should be almost impossible to win. One operator should be able to handle this game.

BUILDING GUIDE FOR PITCH-TILL-YOU-WIN

Materials needed

Plywood
| 1 | 4' x 8' (½") |

Dowels
| 24 | 3' x ½" |

Numbered tags
| 210 |

Wooden hoops

Creating the Gaming Board:

1 Cut the plywood into a 4' x 5' piece.
2 Drill 210 ½-in. holes into the plywood as follows: 14 rows of 15 holes, 2 inches apart, with a border of about 5 inches around all sides.
3 Cut the dowels into 210 pieces, all the same size or varied in height.
4 Glue the dowels into each hole with carpenter's glue.
5 Sand and apply two coats of paint in contrasting, bright colors.
6 Place numbered tags on each dowel rod, so the numbers can be easily seen. (Numbers can correspond either to individual prizes or to categories of prizes.)
7 Set on a sturdy surface for playing.

CHAPTER 9

▼

TARGET GAMES

Ready! Aim! POP! In this part of the carnival, people try their skill with bows and arrows, darts, water pistols, and cork or flock dart rifles to pop a balloon, hit a target, or knock down a miniature dinosaur.

Most of these games are established and proven standbys, though a few are new entries. Here are the games described in this chapter:

Balloon Popper
Dollar Stabber
Poker Bankroll
Wild West Game
Stars and Eyeballs
Safari Game
Spaced-Out Safari
Rolling Eyeballs

In all these games, the sides and back of the booth should be enclosed for safety, to prevent stray darts or other "ammunition" from injuring passers-by. A front counter should completely enclose the area to prevent children from straying into the target area. Experiment to find the best distance from the front counter to the target board so that winning is possible but not too easy. Each booth should also have shelves where prizes are displayed, and a prominent sign that states the cost of play, the rules, and what types of prizes are awarded for each type of win. Darts, pop-guns, and other "play shooters" can be purchased at game supply outlets.

BALLOON POPPER
How It's Played:

Players pay a fee to throw three darts at a big board that is covered with balloons. This game can be played indoors or out. Prizes are determined by the number of balloons that are popped. This is normally a one-person booth. The operator should keep the darts and hand them out to each player before each turn; if darts are left on the counter, there is a tendency to keep losing the supply. I suggest wearing an apron with one side for tickets or change and the other side to hold darts.

This game should have a net profit for the house of 35 to 40 cents for every dollar played.

BUILDING GUIDE FOR BALLOON POPPER
(FIGURE 30)

Materials needed	
Plywood	
1	4' x 8' (½")
Lumber	
2	1" x 3" x 8'
Butt Hinges with screws	
2 pair	2½"

Wood screws
    4   1¼" x #8
Thumb Tacks
Paint
Small balloons (27)
Darts

Creating the Backboard:

1 Sketch an oval on the sheet of plywood. Cut out with a jig saw.
2 Sand and paint, using two coats.

Assembling:

1 Cut the 1 x 3's into three pieces as follows: two 5-ft and one 2-ft.

2 Screw the 2-ft piece to the two 5-ft pieces about 12 inches from the bottom (creating a rough letter "H").
3 Screw one side of the hinge to the top of one 5-ft piece; screw the other side of the hinge about 1 ft. from the top of the oval. Repeat for the other 5-ft piece.
4 Blow up balloons (consider renting or buying an automatic pump for the purpose — unless you have strong lungs). Using thumb tacks, attach the balloons to the board, far enough apart so that they will move in a breeze.

Note: the game can also be made to fit a table top; reduce all dimensions by one-half.

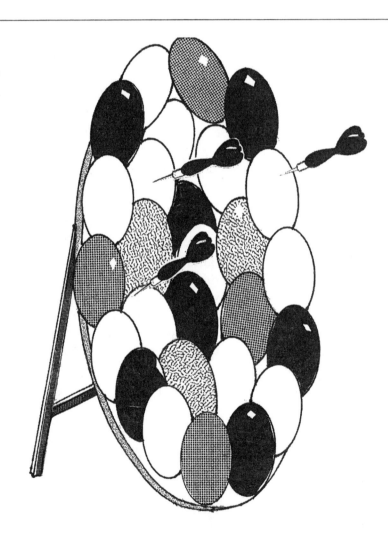

Figure 30. Balloon Popper

DOLLAR STABBER

How It's Played:

Twenties, tens, fives and ones ("funny money" bills) are tacked onto a large board; players throw a certain number of darts and win whatever bill they hit; to win, the dart must hit a bill within the oval portrait printed in the middle of each bill. Because of the high possible winnings, the cost to play this game should be higher than most — at least $1 for throwing three darts.

Note in the illustration of this game, Figure 31, that most of the bills of higher denominations are carefully covered to a great degree by the other bills to make it difficult for a dart to land on a high-value bill. Unless this is done, the game could be a disastrous failure. It is also very important to have sufficient distance between the player's position and the target board so as not to allow too much accuracy. Because of its difficulty, the profit on this game can reach 75 cents on the dollar, but again, because of the high cost to play, there is seldom a large crowd of customers.

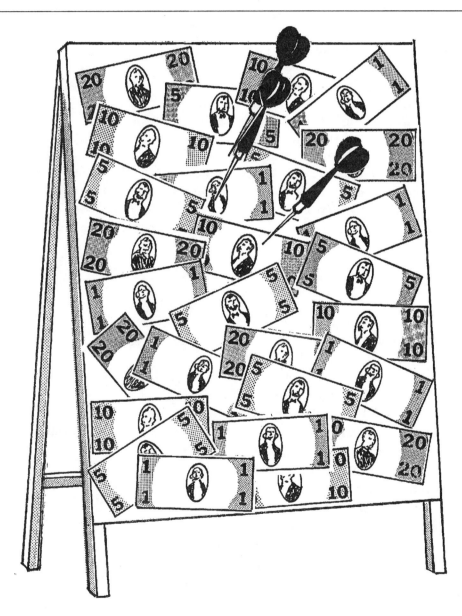

Figure 31. Dollar Stabber

BUILDING GUIDE FOR DOLLAR STABBER (FIGURE 31)

Materials Required

Plywood for board and supports (see
      materials list for *Balloon Popper, pp. 81-82*)
Rubber cement or stapler
"Funny money": about 100 different bills,
      mostly of low denominations
Darts

Building Directions

1 The size of the target board will be determined by (1) the area allowed for the game and (2) whether the board will be set on the floor or ground or whether it will be resting on a table or box.
2 Follow building directions for the *Balloon Popper* (*pp. 82-83*).
3 Sand and paint with two coats of paint.
4 Attach "money" with rubber cement or staples. Rubber cement is preferable, because a dart can be deflected by a staple; also, money that is glued on can be easily replaced. Enough darts should be on hand for more than one player and should be handed out to a player only after receiving money for the play.

POKER BANKROLL

How It's Played:

This game consists of a large rectangular board on which two smaller graduated-size wheels are mounted (see Figure 32). The board and both wheels are covered with playing cards — either regular-sized or photocopied and enlarged. A full deck of 52 cards is used and fastened all over the wheels and the backboard. Before every play, the wheels are spun by the operator, then the player throws five darts and tries to hit five cards adding up to the best poker hand possible.

This is usually a one-operator game, and it is a busy one. The board and wheels can be made in any size, depending upon the size of the booth, whether regular- or oversized cards are used, and whether the board assembly will be freestanding at the back of the booth or

fastened to a stand (a stand provides a bit more stability).

One easy way to display the prizes that apply to each category is to have a separate shelf for each of the listed wins (two pair, full house, etc.) with a specific color attached both to each shelf and to the sign listing that combination. (See the description for *Poker, p. 49*, for winning card combinations.)

Depending upon the kinds of prizes that are given, the game should return at least 50 cents for every dollar played.

BUILDING GUIDE FOR POKER BANKROLL
(FIGURE 32)

Materials needed

Plywood		
1	4' x 8' (½")	
Lumber		
1	1" x 3" x 8'	
Copper tube (bushings)		
2	¼" ID x 9/16	
Threaded rod with 6 washers/nuts		
1	¼" x 6"	
Butt hinge with screws		
1 pair	2½"	
Wood screws		
8	1½" x #6	
Playing cards		
1 Deck		
Rubber cement		

Creating the Backboard:

1 Cut the plywood as follows: one 36" x 42" (for backboard); one 35" x 36" (for base); one 25-in. circle; one 14-in. circle. (*See Big Six Wheel, pp. 9-12*, for instructions on creating a circle.)
2 Drill a 9/32-in. hole in the center of the 36" x 42" backboard and both circles.
3 Using 6 wood screws, attach the backboard perpendicular to, and in the center of, the base piece.
4 Cut the 1 x 3 into two 4-ft pieces. Screw one-half of one hinge to the 4-ft piece and the other to the back of the backboard, about 3 inches in from the side. Do the same on the

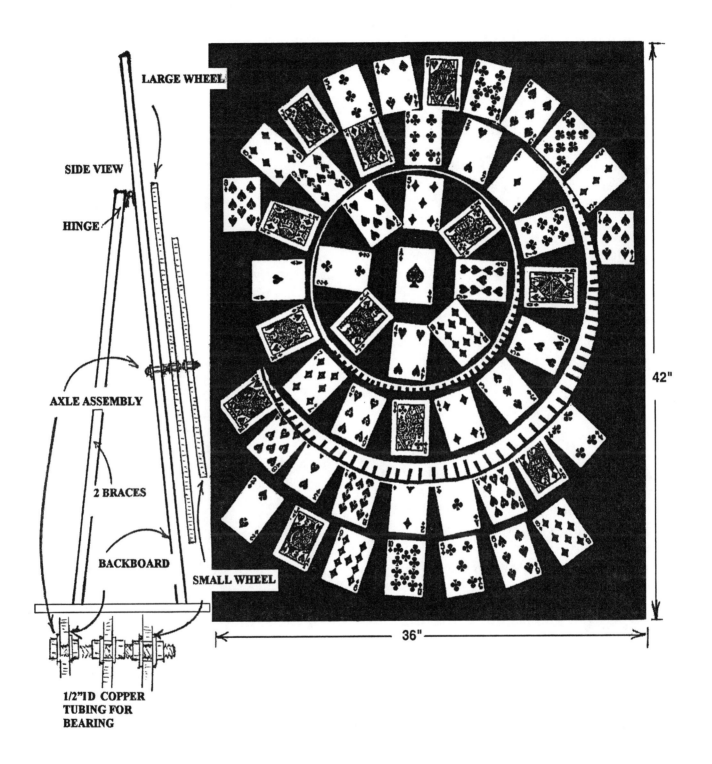

Figure 32. Poker Bankroll

other side, using the second hinge. The bottom of the 1 x 3's should be screwed into the base for stability.

5 Sand and paint this assembly.

Assembling:

1 Thread a nut onto one end of the threaded rod. Add a washer. Insert the threaded rod into the hole in the backboard, adding another washer and nut. Tighten securely.

2 Thread another washer and nut on the rod.

3 Insert the copper tube into the large plywood circle (25"). Place onto the threaded rod. Fix in position with a washer and nut. Tighten. (Be careful not to over tighten, as wheel must move freely.)

4 Insert the second piece of copper tubing into the small circle (14"), and place on the threaded rod. Again, fix in position with a washer and nut. Tighten.

5 Cut off any excess rod with a hack saw.

6 Attach the play cards to the backboard and wheels (as shown in the illustration).

WILD WEST GAME

How It's Played:

This game consists of a two-shelf stand on which 6 cut-out figures of cowboys and Indians are set (see Fig. 33). The object of the game is for players to knock down as many figures as possible with either a bow and arrow or a cork or dart rifle. Because this game is so easy to set up and construct, there can be many variations: for instance, ghosts and goblins for a Halloween bash, or outer space creatures for an event with a "Star Wars" theme.

This game can be handled by a single operator but it may be easier to manage with two: one to pick up the "ammo" — be it darts, corks, or arrows — and righting the fallen figures, and the other to take care of the players.

Depending upon the prizes that are offered and the accuracy of the "weapons," the normal net take on this game should be about 30 cents for every dollar spent.

BUILDING GUIDE FOR WILD WEST GAME
(FIGURE 33)

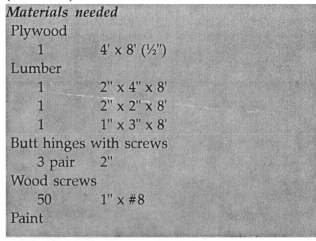

Materials needed	
Plywood	
1	4' x 8' (½")
Lumber	
1	2" x 4" x 8'
1	2" x 2" x 8'
1	1" x 3" x 8'
Butt hinges with screws	
3 pair	2"
Wood screws	
50	1" x #8
Paint	

Creating the Main Assembly:

1 Cut the plywood into a 4-ft square. Mark up 3 inches from the bottom edge and draw a 12" x 40" rectangle. From the upper 40" edge, measure up another 3". Draw a second rectangle 12" x 40". Cut out the two rectangles, saving the 12" x 40"-inch pieces for use later.

2 Cut the 1 x 3 into two 4-ft pieces. Lay them down with the wide side up. With a radial arm or table saw set at a 30⁰ angle, angle cut the top and bottom of each 4-ft piece. Fasten each 4-ft piece on either side of the back of the plywood square using 3 wood screws on each side.

3 Cut the 2 x 4 into two 40-inch pieces. Lay with the wide side up. With a radial arm or table saw set at a 30⁰ angle, cut down the length of each piece (shelf supports).

4 On the plywood square, mark ½" below each space of the cut-out rectangles. Attach the 2 x 4's at these marks using 12 wood screws each; screw inward from the front surface to the back.

5 Using the two 12" x 40" pieces (reserved from earlier), attach above the shelf supports using 10 wood screws each (shelves).

6 Sand and paint.

Creating the Cowboy and Indian Figures:

1 Sketch out three Cowboys and three Indians on the remaining plywood. Cut out with a jig saw.

2 Sand and paint.

3 Attach one-half of a hinge to the rear of each figure. Attach the other half of the hinge to the shelf. Set so that the figures stand upright, but fall backward when hit with a dart or a cork.

STARS & EYEBALLS GAME

How It's Played:

This is a "target within targets" game that presents a challenge to many. The object of the game is to achieve the best possible score by throwing the darts into the highest value targets.

The value on the three targets is decided upon by the game's sponsors. See Figure 34 for a suggestion. Whether to put a value on the stars is also a matter of choice. Going a step further, the shape of the board does not have to be a circle but can be adjusted according to your whim.

Only one operator is needed for this game. Prizes should be selected carefully based upon the expected ease of winning. The expected return on this game should be better than 40 cents on every dollar played.

BUILDING GUIDE FOR STARS AND EYEBALLS (FIGURE 34)

Materials needed	
Plywood	
1	4' x 8' (½")
Lumber	
1	1" x 3" x 8'
Butt hinges and screws	
1 pair	2½"

Creating the Frame:

1 Cut out a 4-ft circle from plywood. (see *Big Six Wheel, pp. 9-12,* for instructions.)
2 Cut the 4-ft section from the 1 x 3.

Figure 33. Wild West Game — front and rear views.

3 Attach one-half of the hinge to the 4-ft piece and the other half of the hinge to the circle, so that the frame will tilt slightly to the rear.

Finishing:

1 Using the figure as a guide, colorfully paint the stars and eyeball pattern.
2 Decide the value of each section and paint with a contrasting color.

SAFARI GAME

How It's Played:

This game earns its name by having various animal figures as targets. Anywhere from three to seven shelves can be constructed and stocked with a colorful assortment of figures for players to choose from. Play rifles that shoot blunt darts are about the best weapon for this game. Prizes should be awarded on the basis of the maximum number of "animals" knocked down by a player.

This game can be run with one or two operators. The profit margin on this game can range around 50 cents on every dollar played if the prizes are selected properly and the targets placed at a correct distance.

BUILDING GUIDE FOR SAFARI GAME
(FIGURE 35)

Materials needed	
Plywood	
1	4' x 8' (½")
Lumber	
5	2" x 12" x 8'
4	2" x 4" x 8'
1	2" x 4" x 12'
Butt hinges with screws	
15 pairs	2"

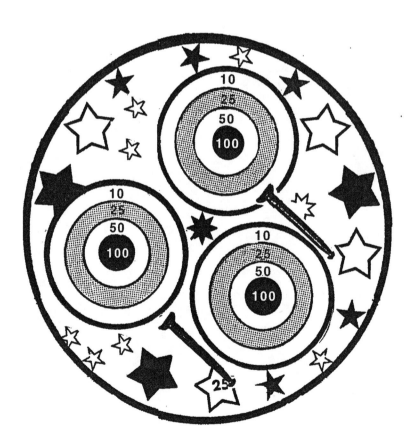

Figure 34. Stars and Eyeballs

Nails
    8   12d common
Wood screws
    44   3" x #10
Toy guns and cork darts
    3 to 6
Paint

Creating the Frame:

1 Cut the four 2 x 4 x 8's to 72 inches.
2 Using the four 72-inch pieces, construct a frame as follows: lay one 2 x 4 down and place another 2 x 4 on top of the first one at an angle of about 30⁰ creating a V-shape. Drive nails through both 2 x 4's. Take the other two 2 x 4's and do the same thing for the other side (supports).
3 Cut the 2 x 4 x 12 to 99 inches. Create a cross-support by screwing to the tops of the face-nailed supports.
4 Take the remaining piece of lumber from the 12-ft piece (about 44 inches), and cut ten 4-inch pieces. (These will be the shelf braces.)
5 Set the frame on a level surface. Starting at the top of the frame, make five marks 14 inches apart down the two front support legs. (This is where your shelves will be placed.) Screw each block to the inside of the support leg on the mark horizontally, checking each block with a level.
6 Cut the five 2 x 12 x 8's to 96 inches. (These will be your shelves.) Screw into place.
7 Sand and paint the frame.

Finishing:

1 Sketch out animal figures on the plywood.

Figure 35. Safari Game

Each figure should be about 8 to 10 inches. Cut out with a jig saw.

2 Sand and paint decoratively.

3 Screw one half of a hinge to the animal figure. Screw the other half of the hinge to the shelf. Do this for each animal figure, being sure that the figure stands upright but can easily fall backwards when hit with a dart.

Note: If you prefer a smaller version of this game, reduce dimensions by half so that the unit will fit on a tabletop. The game operator, with practice, should be able to determine the optimum distance from the game.

SPACED-OUT SAFARI

How It's Played:

This is the moving version of the Safari game. The same principle applies — players try to knock down as many animal targets as possible — but in this version, the targets are mounted on moving circular platforms instead of shelves. Figure 40 shows one version with a cartoon-decorated front frame for added interest. (If your group has the talent or resources, such decorative frames can add color and interest to many of the games described here.)

Operating this game is similar to the stationary version, except that the game has to be shut off after each play to lift the fallen figures in preparation for the next player. The profit margin should be at least ten cents more on every dollar played than on the regular Safari Game, or about 60 cents on every dollar played.

BUILDING GUIDE FOR SPACED-OUT SAFARI (FIGURE 36)

Materials needed

Plywood
3	4' x 8' (½")

PVC pipe
1	4" x 3" Sch 40 (or 80)

PVC pipe base plates
6	4"

Oval-head slotted bolts/washer/nuts
  * ¼" x 1"
(*Note*: to determine quantity needed, count holes in one base plate and multiply by 4 and add 2)
Butt hinges with screws
  15 pair   2"
Electric motor with pigtail and ON-OFF switch or/variable speed switch; Electrical timing motor (which be be purchased at electronic stores)
Pulley (to fit shaft of motor)
Drive belt
Powdered Graphite
PVC cleaner
PVC cement
Paint
Toy guns with darts (about 3 to 6)

Creating the Electrical Assembly:

1 Cut the plywood in three 4-ft circles (see *Big Six Wheel*, pp. 9-12, for instructions), and one 4-ft square, being sure to mark centers first. Label the circles A, B, and C.

2 Mount the PVC base plates to the plywood circles as follows: Mount a base plate on the bottom and top at the center of two circles (A and B) using slotted bolts, washers, and nuts, predrilling holes first. Then mount one base plate on the bottom only of the last circle (C).

3 Take the last base plate, and enlarge center opening slightly using a drum sander on a drill. (The hole needs to be just large enough to allow the PVC pipe to turn freely and not bind.) Once you are satisfied that the hole is correct, mount the base plate to the 4-ft plywood square, predrilling holes first. Mount using slotted bolts, washers, and nuts.

4 Cut the pipe into one 8-inch and two 12-inch sections using a hack saw. Clean all but one end of the 8-inch piece with PVC cleaner. Glue the two 12-inch pieces to the three circles using PVC cement as follows: place one 12-inch pipe in the base plate on the top of circle A. Glue and allow to dry (which will take a few minutes). Take the second

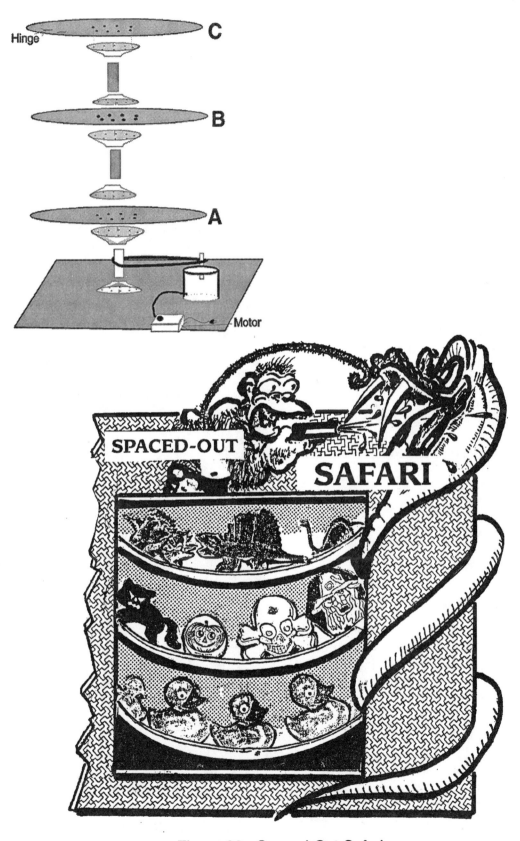

Figure 36 . Spaced-Out Safari

circle (B), and insert the pipe into the bottom plate. Glue and allow to dry. (Now circle A is attached to the bottom of circle B.) Glue the second piece of 12-inch pipe into the top plate of circle B. Allow to dry. Glue the 12-inch pipe from circle B to the bottom of circle C. Allow to dry. Be sure that all three circles are parallel.

5 Mount the pulley onto the motor shaft, using the provided set screws (some pulleys may use other types of shaft mounts). Mount the motor to one corner of the 4-ft square using two bolts, washers, and nuts.

6 Take the 8-inch piece of pipe and notch it as follows: place the 8-inch pipe in the base plate, so it moves freely. Measure the distance between the motor pulley and the plywood base. Measure and mark the corresponding distance on the 8-inch pipe. Using a file, cut a groove around the circumference of the pipe, halfway through the pipe thickness. Place the drive belt in the groove and replace the 8-inch pipe in the base plate, lubricating with the powdered graphite.

7 With PVC cement, glue the top of the 8-inch pipe into the bottom of circle A.

8 Place the drive belt on the motor.

9 Wire the motor to the switch and pigtail. Check electric codes for any special requirements or hire a licensed electrician to do the wiring.

10 Sand and paint.

Finishing:

1 Draw animal figures on the piece of plywood, and cut out with a jig saw. Figures should be about 8 to 10 inches high.

2 Screw one half of hinge to figure and the other half to the edge of the circular platforms. Attach the plastic rim around each circular platform to keep the animals in an upright position.

3 An ornate front (optional) can be used which is screwed into the base with wood screws.

4 An electrical outlet should be available near the booth to supply power to the electrical motor.

ROLLING EYEBALLS
How It's Played:

This game is a mechanized version of the Stars and Eyeballs game. It has three moving targets mounted on a big wheel driven by a constant, slow-speed electric motor; because the three inner wheels are not balanced for proper weight distribution, they will tend to turn as the main wheel changes their positions.

One or two operators are needed to run this game successfully, depending on attendance and demands of the crowd. Profits on the game should run better than 50 cents on every dollar.

BUILDING GUIDE FOR ROLLING EYES
(FIGURE 37)

Materials needed	
Plywood	
1	4' x 8' (½")
Lumber	
1	2" x 4" x 8'
1	1" x 3" x 8'
1	1" x 2" x 8'
Threaded rod	
1	½" x 36"
Copper tube	
4	½" ID x 9/16"
1	½" ID x 1 9/16"
Nuts and Washers	
16	½"
Machine screws, washers, and bolts	
4	¼" x 2"
Pulleys	
2	3"
Drive belt (length will depend on motor mounting)	
Electric motor with pigtail and ON-OFF switch/ or Variable speed switch/Electrical Timing Motor	
Paint	

Creating the Wheel Assembly:

1 Cut the plywood into one 4-ft and three 18-inch circles (targets) (see *Big Six Wheel, pp. 9-12,* for instructions).

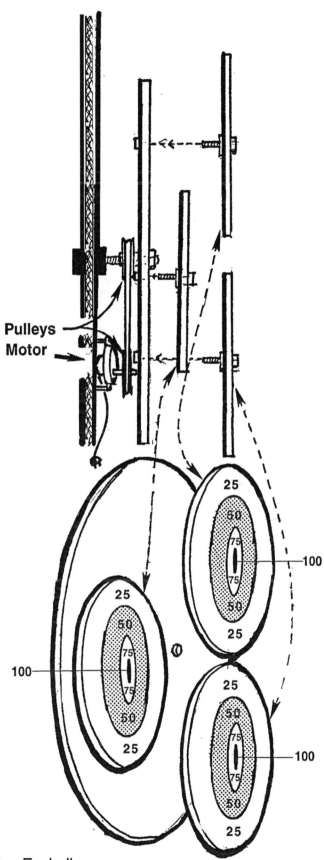

Pulleys
Motor

Figure 37. Rolling Eyeballs

2 Sand, paint, and decorate each of the circles.
3 Construct a stand for the game using the instructions given for the Big Six Wheel.
4 Drill a 9/16-in. hole in the center of all of the circles. Insert a piece of copper tube into each hole. File down the copper tube so that it is flush with the surface of the circle.
5 Drill three ½-in. holes in the large circle at least 18 in. apart (roughly forms a triangular shape).
6 With a hack saw, cut the threaded rod into three 4-in. pieces. Place the threaded rod in the drilled holes and mount the three targets to the large circle, by placing a nut and washer in front and behind each circle. Tighten the nuts on the large circle, but leave the nuts on the targets hand-tight (the targets must spin freely).

Assembling:
1 Drill a ½-in. hole in the stand (2 x 4) 5 ft from the floor. Insert the 1 9/16-in. copper tubing in the drilled hole, enlarging the hole as needed for a snug fit. Insert the threaded rod into the copper tubing. Place a nut and washer in front and back (of the 2 x 4). Tighten, but *do not* over-tighten.
2 Place a pulley on the threaded rod, with the drive belt over it. Put the wheel assembly on the threaded rod, with a washer and nut front and back. Tighten securely.
3 Mount the second pulley on the motor shaft and tighten.
4 Mount the motor on the stand (2 x 4), so that the two pulleys are connected by the drive belt. (Drive belt should be taut between the two pulleys.)
5 Wire the motor to the switch and pigtail. Check electric codes for any special requirements or hire a licensed electrician to do the wiring.

CHAPTER 10

▼

MISCELLANEOUS
GAMES OF SKILL

Here are two additional games to add to your special event. These are standards in the carnival world and easy to construct and operate.

BOTTLE RAISER GAME

How It's Played:

For a change, this is a game that does not require a booth. Its operation and setup are fairly simple and don't require extensive preparation. Players attempt to raise a soda-pop bottle to an upright position using a wooden rod with a string and a wooden hoop attached to the end (see Fig. 38). It's not as easy as it looks! Once the ring slips off the neck of the bottle, if the bottle is still lying on its side, the game is over. If the player manages to raise the bottle to an upright position, he or she wins.

It is not unusual to have a return of better than 40 cents to the house on every dollar played. This game may not attract many players because it lacks the air of excitement that some of the other games do, but it is still worth including in your fair or carnival.

BUILDING GUIDE FOR BOTTLE RAISER GAME (FIGURE 38)

Materials needed

Plywood

1	4' x 8' (½")

Lumber

1	2" x 2" x 10'

Dowels

7	½" x 36"

Wine bottles/or soda bottles (cleaned)

7

Wood rings

7	Large enough to fit easily over bottle necks

Wood screws

18	1" x #6
8	3" x #6

String

Paint

Creating the Gaming Board:

1 Cut the plywood as follows: one 48" x 72" and one 12" x 24". Cut the 12" x 24" piece diagonally (support triangles).

2 Cut the lumber into one 48-in. piece and two 36-in. pieces.

3 Sand and paint all of the pieces.

4 Screw each of the 36-in. pieces perpendicularly to either side of the 48-in. edge of the plywood from underneath, using 3-in. wood screws.

5 Again, using 3-inch screws, attach the 48-in. cross-member to the top of the two 36-in. pieces.

6 Mount the triangular supports to each end

of the plywood base and 36-inch 2 x 2's using nine 1-inch screws per side.

7   Sand and paint assembly.

Finishing:
1   Cut seven 36-inch lengths of string.
2   Tie one end to the dowels and the other end to the wooden rings.

3   Paint.
4   Lay bottles on the platform base.

Note: This game can also be played outdoors without a base. However, the game is more difficult if the bottles are lying on a smooth, flat surface.

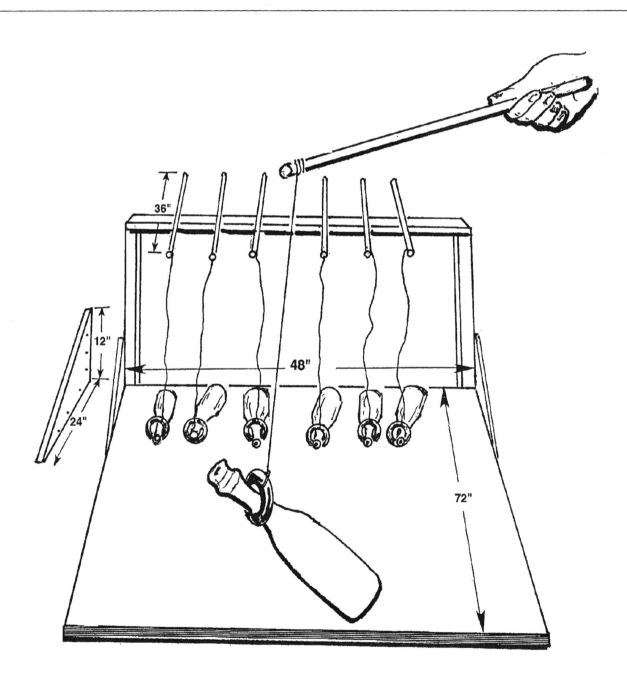

Figure 38. Bottle Raiser

FISH POND GAME

How It's Played:

Frustrated fisherman may or may not vent their wrath in this game of hook, line, and no sinker. Figure 39 shows how this game is set up. For a fee, the player rents a fishing pole fitted with an open safety pin or a bent wire for a hook. The player pokes and maneuvers that hook into a swarm of plastic (or wooden) fish fitted with open rings where the mouth would normally be. The fish can be floating in water, since the tank is usually a small plastic swimming pool; or the tank can be dry and the plastic or wooden fish simply strewn about the bottom. Each fish is numbered corresponding to numbers on the prizes. Since most players will catch a fish each time they play, the prizes should be mostly of very modest cost (a good rule of thumb is that the value of each prize should normally be about half the cost of playing the game). Some better-value prizes may be displayed as an attraction for players to

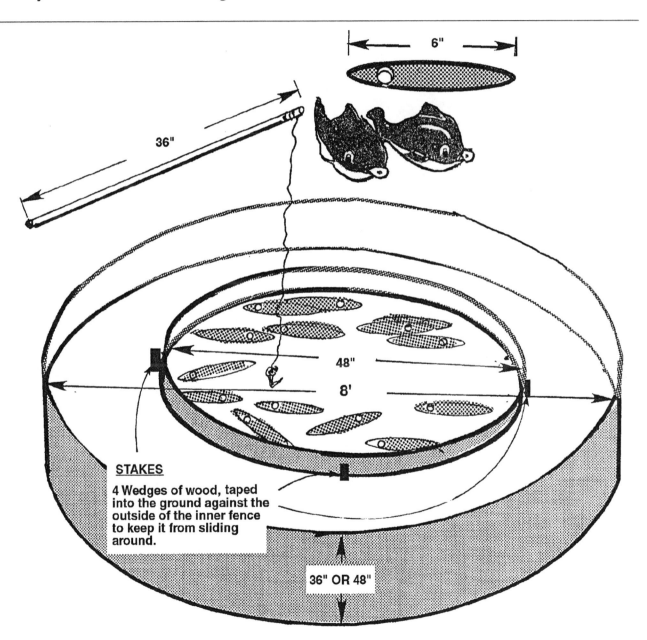

Figure 39. Fish Pond Game

try for, but the operator should devise special precautions so that they are not easily "caught," such as making the mouth openings smaller. (More expensive prizes could also be won by organizing a variation of the game in which several people compete at once in a match to see who can catch a fish first.)

One operator should be able to run this game, and a booth is not necessary. Return on this game should average around 20 cents on every dollar played if steps are taken to have the right stock and control the ease of the players in catching the fish.

BUILDING GUIDE FOR FISH POND GAME
(FIGURE 39)

Materials needed
Fishing poles, made from thin bamboo or wood, at least 4 feet long.
  6
Sturdy string (to attach to the end of the poles)
Safety pins (large) or bent wire (try different guages of wire to find the one that will

pick up the fish you are using without bending)
  6
Plastic fish of various sizes with round loops on the end of their snouts (may be purchased from game supply outlets)
  12 (approximately)
Note: Alternatively, fish can be cut from ½" balsa wood with jig saw or scroll saw and painted.
Plastic "kiddie" pool about 4 ft. in diameter
Larger plastic fence, height about 3 ft., and 10 ft. in diameter

Building Directions:
1 If you are making wooden fish, cut an oval 6" long for each fish, tapering the ends to a point on all sides, and cut a small hole at one end. Sand and paint colorfully.
2 Make the rods by attaching string to one end of the rod and the safety pins or bent wires to the other end. Set up the small pool and fill with water (if using plastic fish), then set up the larger enclosure so that it stands two feet away from the pool on all sides.

SECTION III

AUCTIONS
and RAFFLES

Introduction

To be successful, auctions and raffles depend on many factors. Imagination, good leadership, and efficient organization are some of the most important ones. A great auction has class, generates fun, glows with imagination, and, most of all, is very profitable. Raffles can be very profitable for your organization, especially if a valuable prize has been donated, and will add a lot of excitement to any event.

ORAL AUCTION
(ALSO CALLED A LIVE AUCTION)

This event is set up in a large room or hall with the audience sitting in rows of chairs facing a raised platform or stage on which the auctioneer stands at a lectern. One item at a time is displayed and described, and the auctioneer often suggests a starting bid. Items are sometimes referred to as "lots," and each piece or "lot" is assigned a number for easy identification in a program or display table.

Depending upon the auctioneer's style, the starting bid may be set high or low. Once someone in the audience makes a bid (either by raising his or her hand or raising a numbered card), the auctioneer may verify that he is announcing the correct bid, but this does not always happen. Often, the auctioneer will note the hand up of the person making a bid as he is talking and will automatically assume the bid is right without bothering to check it. He will then keep repeating the bid while urging the rest of the audience to bid a higher sum. Often, he will interject remarks about the high value of the article being auctioned, or about its beauty, its history, or anything he thinks will encourage the audience to offer more money. He will do this for a few minutes, depending on how the audience is reacting in active bidding. When he feels he has reached the maximum amount the audience will bid, he will gradually close the bidding on that item by intoning a familiar phrase: "Going for _____ dollars, once! Going for _____ dollars, twice! Sold to number _____ for _____ dollars!" If his lectern is equipped with a gavel, he may strike once to indicate that the item has been sold and the bidding is over for that item. He then repeats the procedure for every other item until all are sold.

Most oral auctions hold the attention of an audience for about an hour's time. Experience shows that at the end of an hour there is a tendency for an audience to start wandering and gradually begin to lose interest. With this in mind, go over your list of items with your auctioneer carefully so that he's aware of the time span he has to go through the items that will be presented.

SILENT AUCTION

Instead of a room with rows of chairs, this type of auction requires a room to be filled with tables and platforms displaying all the items offered. A card or placard is prominently placed near the item, describing it and stating its dollar value. Sometimes there are several items in a group that are being offered for auction; the entire package should be clearly described. Also, the dollar value is included on the card, based upon the donor's valuation. A bid sheet is placed next to the information card, or on a surface close to the article where it is easy to write. (Adequate lighting is important so that people can clearly see what they are bidding for and what bids have already been made.) The bid sheet consists of a number of blank spaces in which a bidder writes either his or her name or a preassigned number (anonymity sometimes produces higher bids). The next person interested in the item, and wanting to bid, writes his or her name o number in the next space, bidding a higher amount; this same procedure is repeated for

each following bid until the bidding is closed by announcement at some preset time.

RAFFLES

Most events feature a high-ticket item for which it would be very difficult to raise bids high enough to cover the cost. Some examples are a new car or a round-the-world trip. In these cases, a raffle is commonly used. A raffle is set up and sold months in advance (plan on four to six months) so that a large number of tickets can be sold to the general public to cover the cost of the item and make a substantial profit. Often raffle "books" are printed with a number of tickets bound together. Tickets are usually sold individually for one price, for instance, $1 per ticket, and in books of five, ten, or more, for a slightly lower price, for instance, $5 for a book of six tickets, or $10 for 11 tickets. To add to the excitement, more raffle tickets are sold the night of the auction, with regular announcements leading up to the drawing at the high point of the evening.

CHAPTER 11

▼

AUCTION TERMS
AND PERSONNEL

Like most specialized enterprises, auctions have their own vocabulary. Following are some terms and their definitions:

PADDLE NUMBER

As each person enters the auction, a clerk assigns each person a number. This number is written in bold letters on the front of the program each person is given or on a "paddle" (a hand-held sign, usually made from cardboard) large enough to be read by the auctioneer in an oral auction. This number is used for all bidding by the person to whom it is assigned, serves as a record of who won which articles, and facilitates collection of payments.

UNDERWRITING

Underwriters are those people or companies who donate the "goodies" of service and substance to the affair, such as food, beverages, advertising, printing, decorations, location, and so on.

SPOTTERS

Alone, the auctioneer standing at the lectern would have a hard time coping with an active crowd of enthusiastic bidders. He needs "eyes" to spot those hands that, though raised, get lost to his view because of people getting up

and moving or for a multitude of other reasons. Those extra needed "eyes" are a team of alert spotters who are stationed in key areas around the hall to "spot" or point out bidders in their area and signal the auctioneer to be sure he acknowledges their bids. A good rule of thumb is one spotter for every 40 people, but it doesn't hurt to have more if they are available.

RUNNERS

The essential function of these people is to bring the proper items at the correct time to the auctioneer on the platform. They help keep the whole show moving and alive in keeping the crowd interested in the changing scene of auction articles.

CASHIERS AND CLERKS

No event of this magnitude would succeed without the tireless effort and precise organization of those who keep the records of who bought what for how much, and collect the funds with such warmth and efficiency that everyone stays happy and has a good time.

For a successful auction, several committees will be needed. Following are descriptions of the various jobs that need to be performed by a volunteer or team of volunteers:

Auction Chairperson. This person coordinates the efforts of all the other chairpeople and committees. For large events, it also will help to have two co-chairpersons, one for the oral auction and the other for the silent auction, to help coordinate the work of the various subcommittees described below.

Food and Beverage Committee. Always an important section of any gathering. Keeping people well-fed and the beverages flowing freely will contribute greatly to stimulating people to bid more as they have a good time. The food and beverages themselves are often donated, as is the preparing and serving.

Invitations Committee. This group does a lot of writing, calling, and checking to make sure that the auction receives the right number of guests as well as the donors and other key community leaders to benefit the organization the most.

Publicity Committee. The chairperson of this committee should have knowledge of how to best use the news media to publicize your event through public service announcements, advertising (often donated, especially for nonprofit organizations), or any other means available. With this committee working effectively, the results could be overwhelming.

Newsletter and Program Committee. This is a painstaking job that requires a lot of participation and plenty of checking. Publishing the appropriate newsletters at the proper time and putting together a program that is correct in every detail is a formidable job. This should be a busy committee.

Decorations Committee. This group is responsible for all the areas housing the auctions as well as the approaches to them. Not only should decorations be pleasing to the eye but they should excite the other senses, if possible. Proper lighting and ease of movement about the area and displays is important. A creative committee will make the surroundings unusual and exciting.

Music Committee. Music sets an atmosphere that conditions people to be relaxed and comfortable in a pleasant setting with familiar sounds and positive attitudes. Although the music will not be consciously noted by many attending, if it is properly programmed it will have a beneficial effect on the event.

Inventory Control Committee. Definitely a job of staggering proportions. Computer knowledge and use will help greatly to keep track of items and services.

Solicitation Committee. These are the "prospectors" who go out and find the best goods and services for your event.

Sound and Lighting Committee. Unless both these functions run smoothly at the auction, there will be major problems. It is absolutely essential that knowledgeable maintenance people be on hand at the auction at all times in case of a glitch.

Personnel Committee. Someone has to watch over all those hardworking people on all the committees. Problems will crop up. Promises may not be kept; personality clashes do happen; family commitments may alter plans. Many unforeseen and unplanned things may surface.

Correspondence Committee. Someone has to write all those thank-you notes to all the donors and other folks who make the auction a success. As all the other volunteers are telling each other what a tremendous job they did to make this event successful, this committee is putting it all in writing.

CHAPTER 12

▼

SELECTING SUCCESSFUL AUCTION ITEMS

As we've seen in the previous chapter, auctions are a team effort, with many people performing various important tasks. "Prospecting," or finding the best items and services to auction or raffle off, is one of the most important tasks, since this is the "treasure" that the attending public will want to buy.

Even those who are not specifically given the task of being prospectors can help out by helping to identify likely businesses in the community, or even by donating items and services themselves. These may be professional and business people, or simply dedicated people who give something of considerable monetary value to the affair — whether it is a service, a tangible commodity, or both. Some examples of commonly donated items and services mentioned in the previous chapter are food, beverages, and decorations. Other items may be advertising; printing of invitations, ad books, and cards; valet parking service; tables, chairs, and dishes; flowers and shrubs for decoration; and lighting accessories.

Obviously, the more items your group collects for the auction, the more money can be collected overall. However, the actual number of donations you should aim for depends on several factors. For one thing, in an oral or live auction, there will be a certain average time span allotted for the sale of all the items so that

the audience does not get bored (about an hour). In a silent auction, people have to have time enough to visit all the displays and place bids in a leisurely manner, with time for socializing as well, before the final time is called.

Here are a few "do's and don'ts" on how to collect the best items for your event:

Do:

. . . *collect quality items.* Your prospectors should insist on true value in what is being donated. People recognize worth and react accordingly.

. . . *communicate well with everyone.* Take nothing for granted in any conversations with coworkers, donators, service people, or anyone having anything to do with the auction. Your extra effort to be courteous and to double check every arrangement will prevent misunderstandings and impress the community as people will be more likely to donate again.

. . . *package items creatively and impressively.* This is especially important for the silent auction, where the displays will have to sell themselves. Smaller donations can be packaged together as a single article to be auctioned off. Some examples are a "Beauty Time" package consisting of face cream, name brand perfume, and a gift certificate for a service at a local salon. Group items in a lovely decorated basket or display on a satin pillow. Another example is a "Night on the Town" package consisting of limousine service and tickets to a theater. This could be packaged with a model-sized luxury car decorated with a theater program and opera glasses. (Take care, of course, not to neglect your thank-yous to every donor, no matter how small the donation.)

Don't:

. . . *accept "come-on" merchandise or services,* in which buyers would have to spend additional money to claim their prize.

. . . *keep and display items even if they are clearly not suitable for your auction,* due to a poor appearance or some other problem, just because they were donated. Be tactful. Make provisions to return those items to the donors with appreciation for their generosity while explaining that you are unable to use the item for the auction.

CHOOSING THE BEST ITEMS

What's hot and what's not in the world of auctions? You'd better know the answer if you want a good show. Following are some pointers, beginning with a list of some popular items and services commonly seen in auctions. When considering which items to use in the oral auction and which in the silent auction, experience is the best guide. If no one in your organization has run an auction before, it might be wise to consult informally with someone who has. The auctioneer you hire will also be able to tell you which kinds of items are likely to be good sellers in the oral auction. As a general rule, services do better in the silent auction and objects or expensive packages such as a vacation cruise do better in the oral auction.

ATTRACTIVE TRANSPORTATION

New Car. Unquestionably the highlight of any auction. A rare but glorious gift would be to have it donated outright. Next best is to buy it at dealer's cost or under cost. The rule on most cars is to raffle them off, as explained in Chapter 00, rather than sell them at auction, but both methods have been used successfully.

10-Speed Bicycle.

Chauffeured Limousine for a Special Occasion.

Chartered Yacht for a Group Party with Captain & Crew.

Day of Sailing with a Captain & Crew.

Fishing Boat Complete with Captain for the Day.

Golf Cart. Since there are usually many golfers milling around the grounds with the other bidders, this item always gets a big play.

Ride in a Blimp.

Ride in a Hot Air Balloon.

Car Washes for a Year. This could also be listed under "services," but since it has to do with a vehicle, let's leave it here. Naturally, the kids who are often saddled with this unpopular chore will urge their parents to go for this one.

Sailing Lessons

Flying Lessons

SPORTS

Souvenirs. Signed balls or other items from sports celebrities of football, baseball, basketball or hockey are perennially popular at auctions and bring a good bid most of the time.

Celebrity Mementos, such as a tennis star's shoe, a wrestler's robe, or any such oddity.

Pro Partner. An agreement with a professional, such as golf or tennis, to let a bid winner play with him or her — or perhaps an agreement for a lesson.

Tournament Tickets. Tickets to a Super Bowl, World Series, Prize Fight, etc.

Special Sports Night. Transportation to a sports event by limousine and a dinner at a fancy restaurant after the event.

Sport Celebrity Appearance. Have lunch with a sports celebrity or have him or her agree to make an appearance at a special function of your group.

SERVICES

Be sure the statement about the particular service is very specific so that no misunderstanding occurs; for instance, in the lawn service for a year, specify what jobs are included and how often they will be performed.

> Lawn service for a year
> Pool service for a year
> Carpenter for a day
> Plumber for a day
> Electrician for a day

Beauty Time: Present certificates or products for any of the following singly or in combination: haircut/style, facial, manicure, etc.

A Day of Pampering at a Health Spa

Professional Massage at Home

Chef Prepares Dinner at Your Home: Things can't be much better than having a chef come to your home and prepare a delightful dinner for four to six of your friends or family.

Musician, Magician, Clown, Comedian: Any of these entertainers, either alone or in pairs, are great for kid's parties, birthday parties, or other events.

Portrait painted by a well-known artist.

Advertising space in a local or national publication. A real plus to some businesspeople — and there should be plenty of them at the auction.

ANIMALS

Dogs, Cats, etc: Assign someone to walk around the auction area the evening of the event with the pet in their arms. Listen to the oohs and aahs from almost everyone there. You'll be amazed at what people will pay when it comes to the bidding.

VACATIONS

Cruises

Round-trip Air Transportation for Two to a Specific Location. Get the right travel agency and you have it made!

Resort Stay: Be sure to be specific about "black-out" periods and all other the details of what is and what is not included.

Golf or Tennis Package: For the avid followers of either sport, this is a treasure.

Yacht Package for a get-away weekend.

CELEBRITY ITEMS

Souvenirs: Contact celebrities for specific items convincing them of the worthwhile nature of your cause and the value of exposure to the celebrity.

Movie or TV Script

Congressional Favors: Contact your senator or congressman and have him or her arrange to have the name of the winning bidder flown on a flag over the White House and then given to that bidder as a memento.

Disneyworld or Universal Studio Tickets

Season Theater Passes: This should be for a local theater.

Ride on Christmas Float

Politician's Souvenir: Depending on the fame of the person and the public's image of him, this item could be a real money-maker.

ELECTRONICS

Computer

Typewriter

Cellular Telephone

VCR

Camcorder

Video Game

TV

Pinball Machine

Free video rentals for year. Be sure specifics are stated, such as how many tapes at one time, any limit per week, etc.

NO-COST ITEMS

Examples of no-cost items that brought in large bids at a private school auction:

1. The first row of seats for graduation day. ($1,000)
2. Reserved parking space for a student for one year. ($1,500)
3. Dinner for eight at the headmaster's home. ($1,500)
4. A road on school campus named for a family for one year. ($1,200)

And the list of "no-cost" items reaches just as far as your combined imaginations can. Think of the many assets your organization may be able to offer, which if recognized and verbalized can be worth a great deal. Be creative. You'll love yourself for it!

ITEMS TO POLITELY REFUSE

Jewelry: This is too personal an item since tastes vary so widely, and seldom generates enough bidding to cover its actual worth.

Art: Also too personal and subject to individual taste.

Services of professionals such as lawyers, doctors, interior designers and architects. These services seldom sell anywhere close to their worth and usually wind up an awkward embarrassment to both the donor and bidder.

Clothing: Never sells well at auctions. The only exception may be a gift certificate for a complete outfit from a particular store. Pass on the offer of a $25 gift certificate from a store whose outfits start at $250.

Firearms: Forbidden by state and federal law.

GENERAL SUGGESTIONS

Always keep the tone of the whole auction tasteful and classy. Shabby-looking or inappropriate items will tend to downgrade the tone of the event. Avoid items such as exterminating services, male strippers, fortune tellers, cemetery plots, and other things that might seem in poor taste.

ATMOSPHERE AND APPROACH - AN EXAMPLE

An example of the imaginative approach to donated services that is so meaningful to an auction is one that was held for a private school conducted by a parent's association.

The committee contacted a man who had created stage sets for some societies, churches, and a hospital, and who did most of the artwork for other allied public and private projects, to help decorate the hall for one of the auctions. He agreed both to serve as an unpaid decorating consultant and to make specific displays for the auction (the materials for the displays were paid for by the committee). It turned out to be a lengthy process taking better than six months. First, the artist met with the committee to decide on a theme. Based upon the name of the school and some of its origins, the committee wanted a Scottish flavor included in the decorating theme.

The final display featured a Scotch Piper with a balloon taking center position in the hall. Six tartan ribbons trailed from the top of the balloon to six individual displays representing different continents located around the hall. Each display was about six feet high and about four feet wide. All the figures on each of the displays were made of different materials. For instance, the gorilla in the Africa display was built on a frame of chicken wire, with molded styrofoam for the head and chest and wooden hands and feet. A black, longhaired cloth was sewn and stapled to the wire frame. Each display, as it was placed in the hall, was surrounded by donated potted trees and shrubs and carefully lit. An added plus to this fundraiser was that the displays were later sold to a local catering and decorating business for a substantial sum and the proceeds went to the auction fund.

CHAPTER 13

▼

LAYOUT
AND PLANNING

ORAL (LIVE) AUCTION

MINIMUM BIDS - PRO AND CON
Most people with any knowledge of auctions feel that the minimum bid approach is not wise, because of the danger that no one will bid at all, jeopardizing the chances of obtaining any reasonable value for the item. It hobbles the auctioneer, and he will be unable to function normally. It also places the bidders in a restrictive mode and dampens the freewheeling nature of a normal auction. If some donors insist on a minimum bid, it should be set at the absolute lowest price acceptable.

WHEN TO START THE ORAL AUCTION
No one will pay attention to an auctioneer — or anyone else — when they're hungry. It's best to have the auction start after the main course and when the guests are enjoying their coffee and desserts.

WARMING UP
The auctioneer warm ups his audience by beginning with items of an inexpensive but popular nature, such as bicycles, a dinner for two at a nice restaurant, a food gift basket, etc.

TRIPS
The auctioneer should start with the most

expensive. This seems to encourage lively bidding for all the lesser ones.

PLACEMENT OF MOST VALUABLE ITEM
If a new car is being auctioned off, this event should be the high point of the evening and should occur about midpoint of the auction. If there is no new car to bid on, select the most valuable of the prizes for that spot.

PLACEMENT OF LEAST VALUABLE ITEMS
These items should be presented toward the end of the auction, but a less-desirable item should not be the last item.

THE LAST ITEM
The auction should conclude with an upbeat item such as a hot-air balloon trip, Disney World tickets, or something similar. This gives an exhilarating finish to the whole affair, and just about everyone goes away happy.

FLOOR PLAN
Depending upon the available facilities, if both an oral and a silent auction are held, it is best to have a separate hall or room for each (see Fig. 40 and 41). Of course, if this is not possible, one large room or hall can be set up to do double duty.

MAIN AREA GROUPS

The sample floor plan in Figure 40 shows each of the main areas such as Food Service Station, Band Stand, Dance Floor, Clerk's Tables, Raffle Sales Table, Sound & Lighting Control, and Auctioneer's Platform. The diagram also shows 28 tables, all with a good view of the auctioneer's platform; assuming 10 chairs at each table, this plan allows for 280 seated guests. The main item in the auction would be placed prominently in the front of the hall. Another important area to include is space for storage and maintenance work; this area should be screened off from the audience.

DECORATIONS

A pleasing and relaxed atmosphere is very important. A popular and easy decorating motif is potted trees and plants, many of them hung with "twinkle" lights, giving the hall a "fairyland" effect. Though the particular theme doesn't matter, setting the right mood at an auction does contribute to maximum profits. To cite a few actual examples:

A hospital had their fundraising affair in their cafeteria with a circus theme. The "Big Top" was a bed sheet top covering the entire ceiling. The sheets were stitched together by the hospitals' employees. Stuffed animals and doll clowns hung on false trapeze swings from the ceiling. Cutouts of animals were placed around the perimeter of the cafeteria and colorful balloons were strung up everywhere.

A fraternal organization held an auction using a South Sea Island theme. They used both a large and a small hall. In the large hall they draped a dark cloth over the ceiling punctured with small holes to allow the light to appear through like stars. Cutouts of hula girls, dragons, fish, and masks were liberally placed around the hall; there were even palm trees and a "volcano" in one corner, made of papier-maché. Inside was a fan beneath a fine wire basket holding paper confetti and red lights pointed to the open top, creating a spectacular illusion of fire and sparks emerging from the volcano's crater.

At an auction held for a church, a Winter Wonderland theme was held with great success. In the main hall, varying lengths of string with balls of cotton attached were strung from the ceiling about a foot apart. This created a surprising illusion of a snowstorm. Intermixed among the mass of "snow" were giant "snowflakes" cut out from cardboard.

At an affair for a community organization, the theme was a Big Band Bash. In this instance, the auction was held on the private grounds of one of the league's members, an area large enough to accommodate the auction as well as having an area for the guests to park cars. An imposing arch was constructed at the entrance featuring cutouts of familiar band instruments and a dance couple at the apex of the arch and blinking lights surrounding the large lettered message emblazoned across the middle saying,"Big Band Bash." A continuous bubble machine spurted masses of soap bubbles into the air as the guests drove in. The tables were covered with silver and black tablecloths, and centerpieces of original design were in the same colors. All the other support decorations followed the same format.

DINING TABLES

Round tables can be rented in different sizes to accommodate four, six, eight, or ten people seated at each. The basic rule on placing these tables and chairs is to arrange them so that there are no "blind spots." That is, everyone in the audience should have a clear view of the auctioneer at all times. There should be plenty of room so that chairs can be turned around and not obstruct anyone's view.

FOOD SERVICE STATION

All the food and beverage will be delivered and prepared and served from this area. There should be clear and easy access for the people serving the guests, but the area should be fully screened off from the rest of the hall. The guests don't need to be distracted by the hustle and bustle of the kitchen.

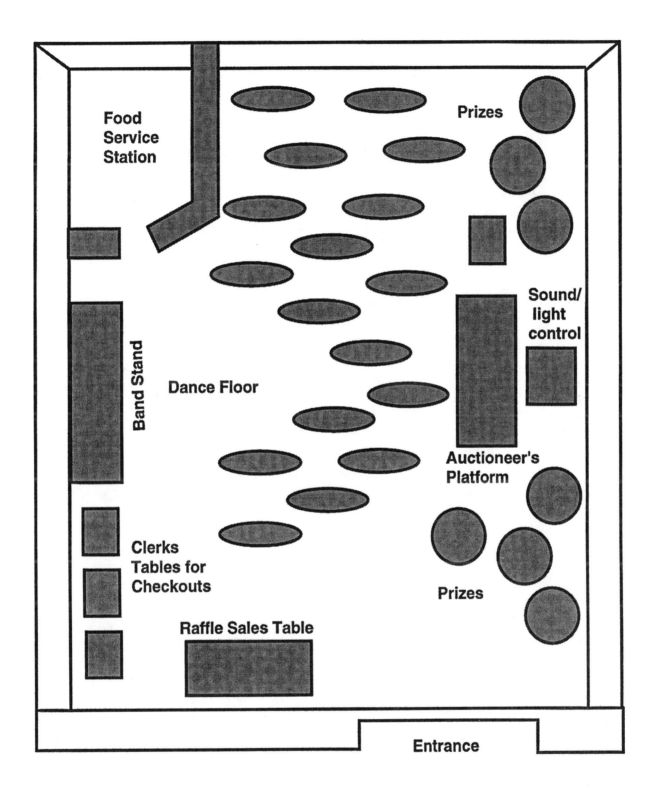

Figure 40. Oral Auction Sample Layout

SILENT AUCTION

FLOOR PLAN

Ideally, the silent auction should be in a separate room or different area from the oral auction. Part of the reasoning behind this is the psychological effect; when the guests enter the oral auction room, they are overwhelmed by the ambiance of the glitter and vitality created by the extensive decorations, captivating displays, sounds of music, and smell of prepared food. It usually puts them into a enthusiastic frame of mind and an excellent mood for bidding.

The silent auction room, on the other hand, is purposely more subdued. Even though the same theme is carried over in this room, the decorations will be in a lesser scale, displays will be less glaring, and music, if there is any, will be on the soft side.

The diagram in Figure 41 illustrates the key areas in a silent auction:

BARS

It's best to have a good number of bar stations around the room so that the guests will then be able to devote most of their time to browsing and writing bids instead of waiting in line for a drink.

GROUPING OF ITEMS

It is best to set up the silent auction room by categories; following are some examples:

Sail Away: A simulated treasure chest filled with bottles of "cheer," boat accessories in a basket or box, world globe on a stand, etc.

Home Sweet Home: Set of durable plastic storage trays, good set of pots and pans, jet spray outfit with sponges, brushes, chamois cloth; power blower for driveways and walk areas, etc.

Body Beautiful: Basket of colognes and related beauty aids; exercise or weight reduction equipment; assortment of health foods in a basket, etc.

Be A Sport: A couple of tennis rackets with balls; Volleyball with goal nets; Camping kit with tent; Boccie Balls set.

Bon Appetit: Basket of spirits; Wine rack; Assortment of fine foods; Gift certificates to restaurants for dinner.

Shopaholics: Assortment of tools; lamp sets; group of figurines or statues; wall decorations or potted plants.

Little Folks: Toy box with toys; baby car seat; wagons or small bikes; video games or box games.

At Your Service: Gift certificates for car washes, beauty salon, health club, lawn service, maid-for-a-day, etc.

Computer World: Gift certificates for free computer lessons; computer paper and box of disks; software.

As indicated in the groupings above, smaller items can be packaged together, such as some wines and foods. Many of the beauty products lend themselves to such combinations and gift certificates for facials, manicures, and haircuts.

TIMING

It is always important to let the bidders know when the bidding time will actually close. Announce the closing time several times during the "bidding period" and give the final warning at least ten minutes before the closing time, stressing the actual time remaining to bid.

Be sure to have a sufficient number of clerks on hand to pick up the bid sheets at the closing deadline.

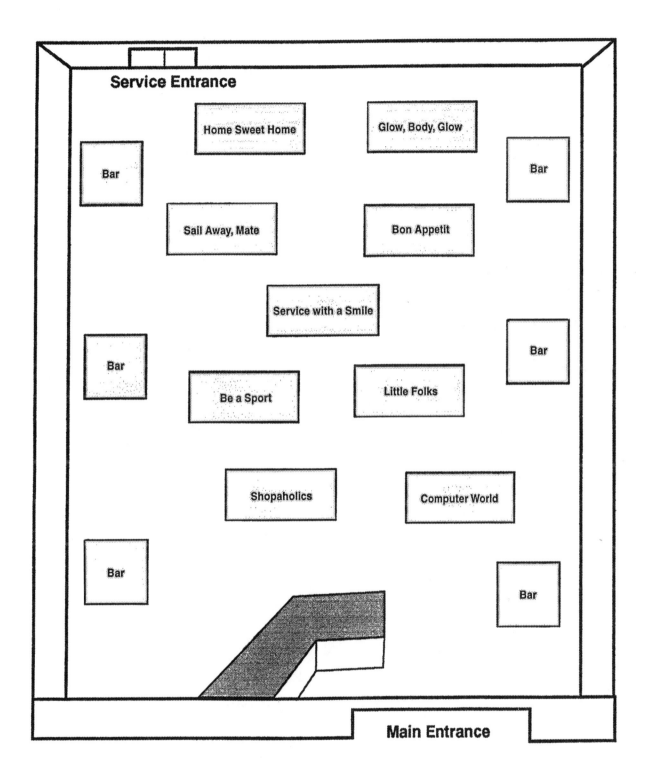

Figure 41. Silent Auction Sample Layout

CHAPTER 14

▼

TIMETABLES

Everything takes time — auctions included. In as complex an event as an auction, careful planning is essential for everyone. It takes a mixture of ideas, experience, and willing people to make a vital successful venture. Here is a formula that has worked for many auctions:

SEVEN MONTHS IN ADVANCE

1. You or someone else associated with your favorite cause suggests an auction as a way to raise funds. You contact some key people or spread the word among members and set up a meeting.

2. At this first meeting, set a date and start thinking about a theme for the auction. Choose the chairpersons for the various committees. Suggest the possibility of a kickoff party to start getting the word around and to build up the excitement.

3. Decide where to hold the auction. If your group is connected with the organization that is to receive the funds and that organization has the facilities (such as a church with a hall, a school with a gym or auditorium, a fraternal organization with large meeting rooms or halls, a hospital with meeting halls or large cafeteria, a civic group with access to public halls or adequate

space), make plans to reserve rooms for the scheduled date and time. Otherwise, begin scouting for hotel hall rentals or other rental possibilities.

4. Start making your contacts with the businesses and individuals who may be donating items for the event. Concentrate on the "no-cost" items. Crank up the imaginations of your "prospectors" and let them soar!

5. Discuss the various materials you will need to have printed to handle the paperwork involved in donations: at the very least you will need a cover letter, an acquisition form, and a donation form. Your cover letter to merchants and donors should explain, very clearly, what your organization is and why it is raising funds.

6. If your group decides to have a special prize or prizes for a raffle, make up the forms for the tickets, decide how many to have printed, and get them to the printer.

7. Make sure you set aside a special fund from your treasury to take care of these initial and ongoing expenses.

FIVE MONTHS IN ADVANCE

1. Secure a place where items for the auction

may be stored. It must be a secure room or area to which only a few key people will have access. All items should be recorded and tagged as they arrive.

2. Solicitation time! This is the rocky road. Often many follow-up calls will be needed to remind donors how important they are to the outcome of this worthy cause and to urge them gently to deliver on their promises to contribute "something really nice." In my experience, a one-time visit is not usually enough.

3. Now is the time to start searching for those marvelous "angels" who contribute their time or expertise or merchandise to serve food, set up tables and chairs, design and build decorations and displays, lend and deliver tons of shrubs and small trees, furnish live music and entertainment, furnish the food or drinks for the event at no cost, print your materials at no cost, and on and on.

4. You will need a catalog for your auction. Start collecting ads from local businesses — either in different display sizes or (to save space) by devoting a section of the catalog to business-card-size ads.

FOUR MONTHS IN ADVANCE

1. The time has come to blow your horn. Use all your resources to put out announcements of every legitimate type, boldly but tastefully. Regular monthly newsletters, in which you describe the items that are coming up for sale, hint at the party plans, and so on, are a "must."

2. Use free publicity opportunities in your local newspaper by submitting articles to the sections having to do with "society" or "upcoming social events." Sometimes an editor may envision a special feature story in your event — the best possible exposure any affair can have. Don't overlook radio and television special events announcements.

3. One of the keys to the success of your affair is to have a capable auctioneer. This is the month to find and hire this person. Try to interview at least three people before hiring someone. Don't gamble on a friend of someone in the group who may or may not have the requisite experience. Amateurs will not make a successful sale.

THREE MONTHS IN ADVANCE

1. Decide on the type of music you want and hire the musicians. Generally this is not difficult: almost everyone can suggest a favorite band in the area that can be hired for an evening. What is important is that the right kind of music is played and that, if possible, the members of the band be attired in outfits fitting with the theme of the auction.

2. Meet with the chairpeople once a week from now on. By this time a lot should be happening, and if it isn't, the auction coordinator should be pushing. This is no time to procrastinate.

3. Plan your menu with the caterers. Be very meticulous. If the affair is being held in a hotel or other rented or donated hall, meet with the people in charge of setting the placements, timetables, menu, and every other item that your group or committee people are not directly involved in personally.

4. Revise or modify the theme of the auction as needed as committees carry through the various phases such as decorations, invitations, lighting and sound effects, and the countless other trivia that always requires attention.

5. Plan the schedule of events for the night of the auction. One suggestion would be to start the hors d'oeuvres and cocktails during the silent auction at 6:30 P.M. Plan for dinner at 8:00 P.M. followed by the oral auction. Winning bids for the Silent Auction are

usually announced just before the Oral Auction starts. Music for dancing can be played after the auction while guests are checking out their purchases with the cashiers. The raffle drawing would be held just before the evening ends.

6. Enter descriptions of the auction items on a computer, or, if one is not available, in a ledger. Descriptions should be brisk and novel with an enticing message that will make people want to bid on them. Here's an example: "Live like a real VIP for an evening! Have a chauffeured limousine arrive at your door and whisk you and your date off to a favorite "IN" restaurant, followed by excellent seats at the Opera. Treat the love of your life to a night she richly deserves."

Four to Six Weeks in Advance

1. Continue meeting once a week with all the heads of committees and anyone else who may have special problems. Try to solve problems as soon as they surface, and smooth any "ruffled feathers" with all the self-control you can muster. Tensions will be rising fast at this point.

2. Have all your invitations and catalogue printed by this time. Invitations should be mailed about a month before the auction.

3. Start full-scale advertising of the event. Newspapers, posters, flyers, newsletters, announcements at get-togethers — use all the resources at your disposal.

Two Weeks in Advance

1. Meetings of the committee chairpersons should be held two or three times a week. Everyone involved should be as fully briefed as possible about what's happening and what needs doing.

2. Flyers or other means of notification should be distributed in the community listing the

items that are included in the auction catalog.

3. Keep in touch with the auctioneer and make sure that he has at least one list of the items to be auctioned.

4. Keep as accurate a count as you can of how many people have responded to the invitations. If returns seem lagging, organize a one-night "phone-a-thon" where just about everyone on any committee is assigned some numbers to call from the list of those who have not responded, to encourage them to attend.

4. Decide how auction items will be transported and unloaded at the auction site.

One or Two Days Before

1. Set up as many props and decorations as possible in the auction area.

2. Check and recheck the facilities for electricity, sound, bathrooms, kitchen, and find out where most of the main switches and shut-offs are. If you're not sure of what to check, assign someone from your group who understands maintenance to do the inquiring.

3. Most likely some items will be submitted for auction at the last minute, after the printing deadline. Have an addendum of these items printed up and attached to the catalog. Make sure the auctioneer is informed about the additions.

The Big Day

1. Assuming your props and decorations are already up, the tables and chairs for the cashiers and clerks need to be set up, auction items put in place, lights and sound equipment set up and tested, trash containers placed about, and extraneous material removed. Constant communication with service people is essential.

2. A guard must to be hired for the day to watch over the items as they are delivered and placed in the area. He needs to remain on duty in the oral auction room while the silent auction is going on.

3. Decide where to store those items that owners want to pick up the next day instead of taking with them the evening of the auction. Arrange to have someone responsible for retrieving the stored items that next day and decide how they will be claimed.

4. Decide what time to have the auctioneer meet with the technical people (electrician, sound man, maintenance people, etc.) to work out details. All of the above should be done as early in the day as possible.

5. Details can make or break your affair. Everything is important. Sound is crucial. Have good professional people who know what they're doing handle all the technical matters. They should be on hand before the auction starts, and they should be close at hand during the auction to make sure everything runs smoothly. Remember that if people can't hear what's going on, the auction will fail. The electrician also has a crucial job: items need to be well-lit in order to be evaluated properly. Musicians and caterers can't function without proper power.

6. Last but not least, arrange for food to be brought in beforehand to feed your volunteers. Hungry people are not happy people, and happy volunteers will go a long way to ensure a successful event.

A FINAL WORD:
WINNING COMBINATIONS

This book has described two very different sorts of events: the fair or carnival, often held during the day with its various "honky-tonk" games, and the auction — usually a more elegant evening event. However, in some circumstances it may be possible to mix different types of functions. Of course there are many variations of each. For instance, often a fair or carnival offers rides and other thrills such as a ferris wheel, roller coaster, fun house with mirrors, and so on. Almost without exception, these rides are contracted out by professionals for such affairs. They come with their own operators who set them up, operate them, and take them down for a percentage of the total take. There is also the possibility of adding food and other concession booths to broaden the scope of the event.

In deciding what other options or mixes to consider, your committee should take into account the size of the event, the type of people who will most likely be attending, the facilities, the budget, and the total number of volunteers available.

Following are descriptions of some events in which the sponsors successfully combined different elements of fairs and auctions in creative ways.

HONKY-TONK & AUCTION

At this combination of a fairway simula-tion plus auction, the affair was held in a social hall with a large adjoining lounge. Opening up to both was a large, modern, commercial kitchen. The skill games were lined up on each side of the hall with a center aisle "fairway" leading from the entryway to a stage on which the auction items were displayed. Some of the games were also set up in the lounge. The kitchen was set up as a food and beverage center for the customers. Music was piped in throughout the hall and lounge during the games and turned off for the auction. Dividing partitions were set up for the game booths that required enclosures, and signs and posters were hung above the booths identifying each game. Many auction items were donated by the members, and many other prizes were donated by local merchants who were approached by the members to participate by giving a gift and having their business advertised at the affair. The auction was handled more simply than is explained in this book, but it still required plenty of preparation. This affair started at 6:30 P.M. Packets of $5000 worth of "funny money" were sold to guests at the entry for $5. With this funny money, guests starting playing the games on the fairway and bought their food and beverages. The games continued until 10:00, at which time prizes were given out to the three guests who had the greatest amounts of "funny money" left. Then the auction began, with three of the members taking turns being the auctioneer. The event ended at about 11:30 P.M. and netted over $2,600.

Honky-tonk, Raffle, & Rides

A church and private school ran this fair in the month of November for five days (including a weekend). The raffle highlight was a Dodge station wagon, for which tickets were sold beginning about six months before the event. There was a large selection of rides, and the honky-tonk games were a mixture of their own and concessionaires'. The same arrangement was worked out for the food and beverage concessions. This is a church and school of over a thousand members, many of whom were active in volunteer work. Since they have extensive grounds, including a ball field, there was ample space for the games, rides and all parking. This is an annual affair and most of the older members are quite familiar with setting up and handling the affair. With all of these positive factors working for them, it should be no surprise that they netted over $101,500 during the five-day fair.

On a Small Scale

Not all fundraising has to do with "big money." There are many small groups in our great country who raise funds in whatever limited way they can. This is especially true of many ethnic groups. The German annual Ocktoberfest is a tradition in many places, as are Italian Festivals and Greek Bazaars. Taking the Ocktoberfests as a model, a Ukrainian congregation of fewer than 100 families decided to hold an affair they called the Autumnfest. It was decided to hold the event for three days:

Friday, Saturday, and Sunday.

Only five booths were put up, and a medium-sized tent was rented for people to play bingo and for a performance of native dances. Canned music was played inside and outside the church, except when a live band played at various times for dancing. Only one game wheel and one game were used. The booths sold bread, cakes, and ceramics made by members. Another booth sold chances on "mystery" prizes that were wrapped in paper and contained sundry small items. Another booth sold native costumes and dolls made by the members. The last booth sold native foods such as a dumplinglike item filled with a potato-and-cheese mixture and rice-stuffed cabbage leaves. In the hall adjoining the church, dinners were cooked and sold, featuring a native sausage, mashed potatoes, vegetables, and bread. A native soup was also served. Pastries of all kinds were also made and sold by the members.

The members also held a raffle, selling tickets beginning about three months before the event. A "50/50" game was held each of the three evenings; members sold chances at a dollar a ticket throughout the evening. At a specified time, a winning number would be drawn; half the money that had been collected was the cash prize. The raffle prize was divided into three cash prizes: $200, $100, and $50. The raffle prizes were pulled on the last evening of the Autumnfest. The result of all this effort was a net profit of over $11,000.

These are only a few of the many winning combinations that can work successfully. All it really takes is a few people with some vision and willingness to work to get it started and watch it grow into greatness.

SOURCES

and

RESOURCES

With a little investigative elbow grease, you can find tons of inexpensive items to use for prizes as well as parts and supplies for building games. You will probably already know some local stores that specialize in discounted or bulk merchandise. To expand your search, check the Yellow Pages of your city directory and those of the nearest large cities (usually available at your local library) under the following headings:

    Games and Game Supplies
    Hobbies
    Crafts
    Building Supplies
    Hardware Stores
    Toy Stores
    Outlet Stores (for discounted or bulk
       merchandise)

To find national suppliers of inexpensive merchandise, or to find out where to rent or buy games or rides too complicated to build, consult the *Thomas Register* a multivolume reference of manufacturers available at your local library. Check under the following headings:

    Toy Parts
    Toys, Plastic
    Watches
    Amusement Park Rides and Equipment

    Carousels
    Ferris Wheels

The following is a listing of source for supplies and equipment for games and carnivals:

Toy parts

John M. Dean, Inc.
P. O. Box 924
26 Mechanics Street
Putnam, CT 06260-0152

Microscale Industries, Inc.
1570 Sunland Lane
Costa Mesa, CA 92626

Brown Wood Products Co.
203 Northfield Road
Northfield, IL 60093

Engineering Labs, Inc.
360 West Oakland Drive
Oakland, NJ 07436

The Rodon Group
2800 Sterling Drive
P. O. Box Drawer 610
Hatfield, PA 19440-0610
(specializing in toy and game parts)

Games and Parts

Game Parts, Inc.
156 Ludlow Avenue
Northvale, NJ 07647

Oakes Enterprises, Inc.
4301 N. West Shores Boulevard
Tampa, FL 33601

Hoffman & Hoffman
P. O. Box 896
Carmen, CA 93921

Yaquinto Printing Co.
4809 S. Westmoreland
Dallas, TX 75237

Kemp Enterprises, Inc.
P. O. Box 824
Farmington, ME 04938

Stuffed Animals and Decorations

Beat It All
7501 142 Avenue N, #654
Largo, FL 34640
(specializing in teddy bears)

Dollcraft Industries, Ltd.
243 Saint Marks Avenue
Brooklyn, NY 11201

Stumps
P. O. Box 305
South Whitley, IN 46787
(specializing in decorations)

Factory Direct Flags & Safety Co.
P. O. Box 61
Hollandale, WI 53544-0147

Games Supplies and Prizes

Comic and Gaming Exchange
8432 W. Oakland Park Boulevard
Sunrise, FL 33345
(954) 742-0777

Bingo King
1660 W. McNab Road
Pompano, FL 33060
(954) 974-4805

Novelty Sales, Inc.
1451 N. Dixie Highway
Oakland Park, FL 33334
(954) 563-5022

Oriental Merchandise Co.
2636 Edenborn Avenue
Metairie, LA 70001
(800) 535-7335

Unique Sales Co.
12714 Nebraska Avenue
Tampa, FL 33601
(800) 456-9464

Carnival Rides and Supplies

Chance Industries
P. O. Box 12328
Witchita, KS 67201

Creative Games
7711 Veterans Boulevard
Metairie, LA 70001

Diversified Assemblies, Inc.
555 Park Avenue E.
Dept. RTM
Mansfield, OH 44901

INDEX

If you enjoyed reading this book, here are some other books from Pineapple Press on related topics. For a complete catalog, write to Pineapple Press, P.O. Box 3899, Sarasota, FL 34230, or call (941) 359-0955.

Keep the Money Coming: A Guide to Annual Fundraising by Christine Graham. Outlines the basic skills needed for annual fundraising for nonprofits, emphasizes strategy and capacity-building — the keys to long-term financial security, and provides charts, check-lists, and guidelines to simplify the processes along the way.

Organizing Special Events and Conferences: A Practical Guide for Busy Volunteers and Staff by Darcy C. Devney. Here is help for anyone who has to produce a public event — from a church social or a school fundraiser to a national conference. Packed with step-by-step instructions, checklists, schedules, this comprehensive and practical guide reveals all the tricks and techniques of the professional event organizer.